THE CRAZY WALL

THE CRAZY WALL

A PLAY IN TWO ACTS

JOHN B. KEANE

THE MERCIER PRESS

DUBLIN and CORK

THE MERCIER PRESS

4 Bridge Street, Cork

25 Lower Abbey Street, Dublin 1

ISBN 085342 389 X

The Crazy Wall had its premiere by the Theatre of the South, Ltd., Cork at the Theatre Royal, Waterford on 27 June 1973 and subsequently opened at the Cork Opera House on 23 July, and Dublin's Gaiety Theatre, 7 May, 1974.

The cast in order of appearance were:

PADDY BARNETT	Gerard Walsh
LELUM BARNETT	Liam O'Mahony
TOM BARNETT	Jim O'Connell
TONY BARNETT	Flor Dullea
MICHAEL BARNETT, N.T., father of the house	Dan Donovan
SEAN TREAN, a carpenter	Chris Sheehan

his friends

JACK STRONG, a shoemaker	Paddy Comerford
LILY O'DEA, the maid of the house	Aine O'Leary
MARY BARNETT, mother of the house	Mairín Morrish
MOSES McCOY, a warderer	James N. Healy

The voice of Lord Haw-Haw was that of
Donal O'Donovan

Production — DAN DONOVAN

Decor — PATRICK MURRAY

Stage Manager — PETER CASEY

To
Paddy Comerford

The scene is set in the back garden of Michael Barnett's house in the small town of Lolinn in the South of Ireland

ACT ONE

ACT TWO

This scene will take place before the action of the play itself begins. It is not a part of the play but it may be necessary to complement the story. The grass-covered ruins of a fallen wall are to be seen at one side. About there are some shrubs and bushes. It is much the same as in the play itself except that some time has passed.

(Enter three young men. They are Paddy, Tom and Lelum Barnett. They wear black armbands).

PADDY: It's a long time now since we were all together here.

LELUM: It's not that long. You were young then. It just seems a long time. *(Lelum moves away and stands with his back turned, looking into nothingness).*

PADDY: We had good times.

TOM: They were sad times.

PADDY: Of course they were but by and large they were great old days.

TOM: It's a pity we had to break up when we did.

LELUM: *(Without turning)* All families break up. Everything breaks given enough time.

(Paddy and Tom exchange looks).

PADDY: *(Unloosing armband)* I suppose we had better take these things off.

TOM: Yes . . . They serve no purpose now.

PADDY: Will I take your band Lelum?

LELUM: *(Without turning)* No. I'll leave it on a while yet.

PADDY: Let's all leave them on then.

(Enter Tony Barnett in the uniform of an army officer. He bears a tray on which is a bottle of whiskey and some glasses).

TOM: How's mother?

TONY: The girls are with her. She'll be alright.

(Tony pours whiskey into four glasses and hands them round).

9

TOM: I was trying to recall as we stood by the grave-side when was the last time the four of us were together in this place.

TONY: The war was at it's height. That's a clue to begin with.

PADDY: Let's toast the memory of the man we buried to-day.

LELUM: (*Turning*) Yes. A toast.

PADDY: Don't you think you had better explain?

LELUM: Explain. To whom?

PADDY: To the world and to those who might be out there in the dark.

LELUM: Yes. I'd better (*to audience*) We buried our father to-day and so we toast his memory.
(*All quaff. As one they turn and fling their empty glasses against the ruins of the wall. The glasses smash to pieces. All four turn and face audience. Tony salutes*).

TONY: Amen.

OTHERS: Amen.

PADDY: To outsiders he must have seemed a very average man. He was anything but.

LELUM: I remember when it was that we four last stood here. It was the time of Adolf, an evil star of great magnitude whose ascendancy was brief yet long enough to bewitch his nation of Germans and stifle forever the cries of millions of mankind.

PADDY: It was the time of Musso the Wop as the British called him or Benito as his wife called him.

TOM: It was the time of Franklin Delano and Winston.

PADDY: It was the hour of Alexander and Eisenhower and Rommel and Hess, poor fellow, who is still imprisoned at the pleasure of the wretches far worse than he.

LELUM: This is how history will remember it. Principally I think, when all the chaff is sifted, it will be the time of Adolf.

PADDY: But not for us four.

TONY: Oh by God no!

LELUM: For us it was the time of the crazy wall.

PADDY: That heap you see behind us.

LELUM: Erected by the man we buried to-day.

PADDY: Europe had it's war but we had a drama here as good as any and for us the most important drama of all.

LELUM: It made us what we are to-day.

TOM: The precise time we stood here together.

PADDY: Was not the night of the long knives.

LELUM: It was the night of the crazy wall.

PADDY: Judge for yourself.

LELUM: In the light of recent developments.

PADDY: Which was the more important?

LELUM: The rise and fall of the third Reich.

ALL: Or the rise and fall of the Crazy Wall.

TONY: Tenshun! (*They snap to attention*).

TONY: By the left quick march! (*All march off*).

CURTAIN

SCENE 2

The time is May of nineteen forty three. It is the late afternoon. The action takes place in the back garden of a house in the small town of Lolinn in the south of Ireland. It is a colourful and unruly garden with part of the scullery of the house showing at the left facing the audience. At the other side of the stage is an old table on which are scattered some old paint tins, odds and ends and a fairly large wireless set. Most of the area is ivy-covered. Enter a young man of twenty or so. He turns wireless dial and flops on to an old garden seat nearby. He is of the house. He is the second oldest son Lelum Barnett. There is a loud crackling from the wireless but this is superceded by the lively martial music of a brass band. Lelum rises suddenly and comes to attention. He salutes stiffly and marches about like a soldier on parade. He suddenly halts and shakes his head. From one of the shrubs he selects a flower at random, smells it, fondles it and places it in his lapel. He returns to his seat where he sits with his head in his hands. The music ceases.

LELUM: (*Perfectly mimicking voice which follows*) Station Bremen, Station Bremen, Germany calling, Germany calling.

HAW-HAW: Station Bremen, Station Bremen, Germany calling, Germany calling.

(*Lelum Barnett sits erect and listens*).

HAW-HAW: One must accord tremendous respect to the imagination of those who prepare the news bulletins in the B.B.C. For instance the report that the entire German army capitulated in Stalingrad is completely without foundation . . .

(*Enter Michael Barnett, father of Lelum. He is a man of fifty-five, well dressed. He is followed by two cronies. One is bowler-hatted and sharp-faced. He is moustached and nattily dressed. He swings a walking cane carelessly. He is of the same age. He is Jack Strong. The third man is Sean Trean. He is also of the same age. He is a strong, serious-faced man who wears the collar of his shirt outside his coat. Generally stands with his hands behind his back, head erect, legs apart. Michael and Sean Trean wear green armbands; these to denote that they are members of the local security forces. All three would seem to be somewhat intoxicated. Their conversation ends abruptly upon their awareness of Haw-Haw. Michael Barnett lifts a hand for silence. All three range themselves around the table where the wireless sits, having refused the offer of a seat from Lelum*).

HAW-HAW: (*Continuing*) The Fuehrer does not deny

that a small part of the German army capitulated but the truth is that the main body of the army has left the Eastern Front for the following reasons. It is an area not worth contesting in the light of new developments. The Russian Front was never a priority with the Fuehrer. Like the British army the Rusians can be beaten at any time.

SEAN TREAN: Hear, hear.

(*Michael Barnett motions for silence*).

HAW-HAW: While the British Army plays ducks and drakes in Tunisia the German Army occupies itself with more important developments. The truth about the British Army is that it would not beat the tinkers out of Rathkeale on a fair day.

SEAN TREAN: (*Beside himself*) Beautiful, beautiful. (*To Jack Strong*). Did you hear that! The British Army wouldn't beat the tinkers out of Rathkeale.

MICHAEL: Will you please desist or I'll turn off the damned thing.

HAW-HAW: Earlier today the Luftwaffe successfully bombed all the major English citics. Nothing shall withstand the might of the Third Reich. It will stand for a thousand years. The invincibility of German military power . . .

MICHAEL: Turn it off Lelum.

(*Lelum rises and does as he is told*).

MICHAEL: What are you doing inside on a fine day like this?

LELUM: I got fed-up walking around. There's nothing to do, nowhere to go.

MICHAEL: You could get a job.

LELUM: There are no jobs.

MICHAEL: (*To cronies*) I don't know what I'll do with him. There's Tony my eldest in the army, our own army. A credit to his family and to his country. There's Tom and Paddy at school, solid and predictable, and here's Lelum not knowing in God's name what he wants.

JACK: You must give him time. You can't put an old head on young shoulders.

SEAN: That's a fact. We were all like him once.

MICHAEL: If you wait another year I might manage to send you to the university.

LELUM: I've already waited a year.

SEAN TREAN: You could join the army. It wouldn't be for long.

LELUM: Which army?

SEAN TREAN: The Irish army of course.

JACK: The British would be better. At least they're fighting for something.

LELUM: They're all the bloody same. They're all fighting for their suppers. A soldier does what he's told, not what he believes.

SEAN: (*Indicates his green armband*) You could join the Local Security Force like us.

(*Lelum and Jack Strong laugh*).

MICHAEL: Laugh if you will but we have a role to play too.

JACK: What role?

LELUM: (*To Jack*) Did you ever sit down and ask yourself what guarantees our neutrality.

JACK: Well . . . no. Not really.

MICHAEL: The presence of American troops in the North guarantees it. The proximity of England guarantees it.

SEAN: The Germans respect our neutrality.

JACK: The Nazis respect nothing.

MICHAEL: We have an army of our own remember, never stronger than it is right now.

LELUM: (*To Jack*) Did you ever ask yourself why the Russians never bother us, why England didn't take us over long ago, why the Yanks don't put an army of occupation in here? Think . . . Use your imagination . . .

JACK: (*Pretending to let the truth dawn*) (*Touches band on Sean's arm*) It couldn't be. You mean . . .

14

LELUM: What else? It's the green band of our Local Security Force my friend. That little band, small as it may be, strikes terror into the heart of every army in Europe. While men like these wear bands like those the freedom of small nations is assured. There's hope for the world, hope for us all. (*Raises his hand to salute while Jack Strong allows his hands to simulate a trumpet. He plays gently into it . . . The Last Post. Sean Trean is not at all certain but that they are serious*).

MICHAEL: Stop this nonsense at once. I'm ashamed of you Lelum. I have half a mind to strike you. And you Jack . . . you should know better.

JACK: Sorry Michael. It was a poor joke. I am sorry.

MICHAEL: You Lelum? Are you sorry?

LELUM: If that's what you want me to be.

MICHAEL: But aren't you sorry off your own bat?

LELUM: Alright. I'm sorry.

SEANH The two of you should be ashamed of yourselves. You mock your own country when you mock these bands.

MICHAEL: Only the Irish have this peculiar ability. It's a quirk in our characters I can never fathom, this deep-rooted shame of each other's virtues, this urge to pull each other down, this mad desire to disrupt anything that's decent and good so long as it's a creation of our own. It's held us back for too long. I'm afraid it will always divide us.

LELUM: I said I was sorry didn't I.

JACK: A bit of criticism does no harm.

SEAN TREAN: Not that kind of criticism. It's no fun when our country is besmirched. Our uniforms must be revered and respected.

MICHAEL: Easy Sean. You'll go too far the other way. That's another national failing, taking ourselves too seriously. It's hard to know which is worse . . . too little patriotism or too much.

JACK: The less the better.

SEAN: The more the merrier.

MICHAEL: Enough now. Let's get down to the business that brought us here.

JACK: Before we do . . . I think I could fix you up Lelum with a job on the County Council. It's the time of the turf-cutting and they're taking on seasonal workers. Would you be interested?

LELUM: I suppose I would.

JACK: The money's good.

LELUM: In that case I'm your man. I never had enough money in my life.

MICHAEL: Neither had I if that's what you mean. I was always short.

LELUM: Well it wasn't from giving it to me you were short.

MICHAEL: About your business now like a good boy. We have important matters to discuss.

LELUM: How is it you never seem to be short the price of a drink?

(Exit Lelum)

MICHAEL: How does one deal with a boy like that?

JACK: He's gone from being a boy. We shouldn't lose sight of that.

MICHAEL: Still that's no way to talk to his father.

SEAN: That's the new generation. They're all the same. My eldest daughter is smoking cigarettes.

JACK: But she's a qualified nurse. She's a wage earner.

SEAN: I don't care what she is. She shouldn't smoke opposite her father.

MICHAEL: He's right Jack. There must be respect for authority. A line must be drawn somewhere otherwise our children could turn into dictators. But enough . . . let's get down to the business in hand.

JACK: Maybe if you told us exactly what you had in mind we would be better able to advise.

MICHAEL: For years now, in fact since the day I was born, I've endured all kinds of trespass from neighbours, strangers, friend and foe alike. This could have been a really beautiful garden, a show-piece but let me plant a shrub or a bed of flowers and every bloody stray ass, mule and horse in the countryside will turn up to wreck my best efforts. Take Hanratty's hens alone. The amount of damage they've done in the past twenty five years must run into hundreds. I wouldn't mind that but if there's a bit of rivalry over a new pullet this is the arena for every cock-fight in the bloody street. Before I go any further I would like to ask you both a question and I expect an honest answer. Am I a man that looks for trouble?

SEAN: I should say not.

JACK: A quieter man never drew breath.

MICHAEL: Have I ever gone out of my way to provoke any person?

BOTH: No.

MICHAEL: Have I ever deliberately gone in search of trouble.

SEAN: Never.

MICHAEL: I've tried peaceful means. I've spoken to Mrs. Hanratty a thousand times. I've tried to reason with the owners of strayways. I put up a sign . . . Trespassers will be prosecuted. I tried lettuce wire and thorny wire. All torn down. Well to come to the heel of the matter this is what I've decided. I intend to build a wall from here to here. It's the only solution.

JACK: What does the wife say?

MICHAEL: She approves but even if she objected the wall would still go up. I intend to start right away but before I do I would like to hear your opinions. You're both tradesmen. You are also my lifelong friends.

SEAN: There is no doubt but you've suffered your share. I think you're doing the right thing. You're entitled to your privacy as much as any other man.

MICHAEL: Well Jack?

JACK: Yes, yes, you have the right. There's no gain-saying that. The bother is will it stop at one wall.

MICHAEL: How do you mean?

JACK: One wall could lead to another if you know what I mean.

MICHAEL: I don't know what you mean.

JACK: You build a wall. You give everybody else a licence to do the same. Soon the whole street will be full of walls. You build a wall and you keep out Hanratty's hens. You shut out stray asses, mules and horses but you also shut yourself in. Building a wall is a very serious matter. I'll concede you'll keep out undesirables. You'll have more peace and privacy but you'll also be shutting out certain other things.

MICHAEL: What other things?

JACK: Wandering tramps, children, dogs. Even neighbours, lots of things.

MICHAEL: Have you an alternative?

JACK: No.

MICHAEL: Nobody will deny that I have tried every other means. I've been the very soul of reason. I have been patient. I've been tolerant. There is only one thing left and that's a wall.

JACK: If your mind is made up then you better build it. I don't know much about walls. I'm only a part-time shoemaker but one thing I will tell you. If you must build a wall build a right wall. Build something that will last.

MICHAEL: I intend to. I intend to build a wall that will be standing here when our names are forgotten, a wall that will still be proof against all weathers. A wall that will stand firm and strong and indestructable when the mounds of our graves have sunk beneath the green grass. A hundred years from now a man will stop here and look and say to himself "Christ Almighty but they could build walls in those days". That's the kind of wall I propose to build.

JACK: But you know nothing about building walls.

18

MICHAEL: I know enough.

JACK: Your best bet would be to employ a stone mason.

MICHAEL: I have no intention of employing anybody. If I can't build a simple wall after all these years then my mission in life is a failure. You are a carpenter Sean. Tell him how easy it is to build a wall.

SEAN: Well it's easier than hanging a door. I believe the whole secret about building a successful wall lies in the foundation. It's like anything. Without a foundation nothing lasts. You dig a proper foundation and you're on your way towards the building of a wall that will stand up for generations to come. A weak foundation will be swept away with the first rainstorm. A shallow foundation and your wall will fall before the first decent gale of wind. A wide and deep foundation and you'll have a wall that no man need be ashamed of.

MICHAEL: I see what you mean. You know more than you pretend Sean.

JACK: Will you lay blocks or do you propose to shore it up with boards?

MICHAEL: No blocks for me. Who would guarantee their quality? No. I'll shore it up with boards. I'll mix the gravel and cement myself.

SEAN: Make sure your gravel is well washed and of good quality. Make sure your cement is fine and dry. Make certain your level is accurate.

MICHAEL: You're a deep one.

JACK: He seems to know walls.

MICHAEL: There is no part of the Atlantic ocean as deep as that man.

SEAN: Just a few simple precautions, that's all.

JACK: When will you start?

MICHAEL: I'll begin tomorrow. After school I'll open the foundations. Has anybody any other suggestions?

JACK: I think another drink would be in order.

MICHAEL: I couldn't agree with you more. What do you say Sean?

19

SEAN: It would be no more than fitting. The wall will have to be properly baptised.

MICHAEL: This will be a wall to remember. I can't recall being so anxious to get started with any project.
(*Enter a young girl, hardly twenty. She is Lily O'Dea. She wears an apron over her frock*).

MICHAEL: Yes Lily. What is it?

LILY: The missus wants to see you master.

MICHAEL: Any idea what it's about Lily?

LILY: I think it's about Tom and Paddy master.

MICHAEL: Are they home from school?

LILY: They just come in now master.

MICHAEL: Tell the missus to come out here Lily. Tell her my friends are here. She'll understand.

LILY: Yes master.
(*Exit Lily*).

MICHAEL: Whenever I get started on a new scheme something always crops up to get in the way. Nothing is going to get in the way this time. No matter what, this wall is going to be built.

JACK: We can go on and you can join us later if you like.

MICHAEL: Not at all. This won't take a minute.
(*Enter Michael's wife, Mary Barnett. She's an attractive middle-aged woman. She is followed by two young men, her sons, Tom the older* (19) *and Paddy* (18). *Both carry large, strapped bundles of school books*).

MICHAEL: What's all this in aid of?

MARY: You can prepare yourself for a shock. Your two fine sons are a nice reflection on the household.
(*Lelum and Lily sidle in and range themselves in the background. Jack Strong and Sean busy themselves elsewhere on stage. Sean produces a cord, one end of which he hands to Jack. They measure distances, make calculations, etc.*).

LELUM: What have they done?

20

MARY: You'll find out. Just read that. It's from Father Cartney, the president of Saint Martin's.

MICHAEL: What does that fool want? Damn well you know I don't speak to him.

MARY: The letter is addressed to me but it concerns you more than any of us.

(*Reluctantly he accepts letter, he examines it*).

MICHAEL: I can't read this. It's worse than a bloody doctor's prescription. (*To Lelum*) Here. You read it. (*Lelum accepts letter*).

LELUM: (*Reading*) Dear Mrs. Barnett, it is with reluctance and regret but primarily because of a sense of duty that I take my pen in hand to acquaint you of the doings of your sons, Thomas and Patrick. As you know Tom sits for his leaving certificate this coming June and Patrick next year. Tom's teachers inform me that he cannot and will not keep his eyes open during classes. He has been warned repeatedly and only yesterday fell fast asleep during the history class. At first we foolishly believed that these bouts of sleep might be due to the fact that he was burning the midnight oil in his home but the real reason came to light at two o'clock this morning. The senior curate of the parish, Father Barnum, for some weeks now has been repeatedly informed that some young local girls and soldiers from the new barracks are misconducting themselves in Hanratty's shed.

MICHAEL: Misconducting themselves? What does he mean? Why isn't he more explicit. Misconducting themselves indeed. That could mean anything from piddling in public to free-handed fornication.

MARY: Will you please let Lelum read on.

MICHAEL: It's a wonder the oul' gasbag wouldn't call a spade a spade.

MARY: Go on Lelum.

LELUM: (*Reads on*) Father Barnum lay in hiding for awhile and when he heard singing and laughter in the shed he decided to inform Mister and Mrs.

Hanratty. The Hanratty's with the aid of a storm lamp and accompanied by Father Barnum entered the shed unannounced and witnessed a number of local serving girls lying in the hay with soldiers. Also in the shed was your son Thomas who stands for his leaving certificate this year. He had his arms around a girl. He ran off when the light was shone on him, knocking Mrs. Hanratty to the ground. This in itself was just one offence and, serious as it was, might be overlooked on his undertaking to turn over a completely new leaf but the simple truth is that he goes to the shed repeatedly and according to Mrs. Hanratty his voice can be heard clearly above all the others at all hours of the morning.

MICHAEL: Is this true Tom— . . . Is it true? For the last time Tom is it true?

TOM: Yes.

MICHAEL: But what about your exam?

TOM: I'm sorry dad.

MICHAEL: But how did you get out of the house? The front and back doors were locked and bolted.

TOM: I tied a rope to the leg of the bed and scaled down the front of the house.

LELUM: The call of the wild.

MICHAEL: You shut up. Tom this is a terrible admission. You've betrayed us all, me, your mother, your brothers and sisters. You've cheapened us in the eyes of our neighbours and disgraced yourself. We pay dearly for your education. We feed and clothe you and this is how you repay us. I don't know what to say to you. Nothing I could do to you would be punishment enough.

MARY: He should be whipped and kicked 'till his bones ache. He deserves nothing but contempt. 'Twill be many a long day before I speak to him again.

LELUM: What have you to say for yourself?

TOM: I'm sorry.

MARY: If he says that once more I'll split him.

22

TOM: (*Anguish*) What else can I say? I'm sorry. I'm really sorry that I should disgrace you all.

MICHAEL: Go to bed Tom.

(*Tom bends to collect his books*).

MICHAEL: Leave your books. Go to bed and stay in your room until I call you.

(*Tom is about to exit*).

TOM: Can I have my supper before I go?

MICHAEL: (*Suddenly losing temper*) Jesus I'll give you supper in the arse if you don't move out of here fast.

(*As he advances upon Tom the latter exits hastily*).

MARY: Is that all?

MICHAEL: That's all for now.

MARY: Get your walking stick and go after him. Beat him within an inch of his life. He deserves it. Go after him and beat him. That's what he understands.

MICHAEL: It's not over yet. I'll deal with him later.

MARY: Later, later. It's always later. One day it will be too late. Well he's not going to escape me. If you don't beat him I will.

(*She seizes a stick from table and exits*). (*She is followed by a gasping Lily*).

MICHAEL: (*Futilely follows her a few paces*). Now, now Mary. You mustn't upset yourself. Beating him will achieve nothing. (*He turns away hopelessly*) Why did it have to be our Tom. Just when everything was going so smoothly. Just when I thought I was on top of the world. We never know what's in store for us from one minute to the next.

JACK: Don't let it upset you Michael. The rearing of a family has it's ups and downs.

SEAN: That's the truth. If you could remember that it's only all going through life. That it will even itself out in the end. What seems awful now will be nothing in the course of time.

JACK: For every bad day there's a good day.

SEAN: For every frown there's a smile.

23

JACK: For every tear a laugh. It's the balance of life.

MICHAEL: You're a consolation boys. A pure consolation. That boy was reared better than any in the street and what good does it do? (*He notices Paddy and remembers that he too is mentioned in dispatches*). And pray what perversion has this misbegotten wretch perpetrated when our backs were turned?

LELUM: (*Lifts letter aloft and laughs*). This is absolutely priceless. This is the sort of thing that belongs in Hans Andersen. This is the sort of thing that could happen only to a product of this environment — In short my dear father it could only happen to a son begotten by you.

MICHAEL: Read the letter and pass no comment.

LELUM: (*Reads*) Consequently for the good of the class I am suspending your son Thomas Barnett for a period of one week.

MICHAEL: I see nothing priceless about that. That's bloody hard luck with his exam only a month away.

LELUM: It's not that. It's our friend here.

MICHAEL: What about him?

LELUM: (*Reads*) So much for your son Thomas and I am indeed sorry Mrs. Barnett that the suspension has to take place. For the sake of good order in the school I have no other course open to me. With regard to the younger boy Paddy I don't quite know where to begin. In the middle of his Greek class less than a month ago he excused himself and went outside presumably to answer a call of nature. When he did not return after a quarter of an hour his teacher became suspicious and decided to investigate. He found your son Paddy talking to himself on the elevated stone steps near the lavatory at the rear of the school. When asked what he was doing he replied that he was invoking the aid of the Holy Ghost as he was about to embark on the writing of an epic poem. Since then his teachers can get no good out of him. He has been warned repeatedly. His final exam comes up next year as you know and this is hardly the type of groundwork that is conducive to good results. Rather than suspend him I would ask you and his father to speak to him and point out to him the error of his ways. I am indeed astonished at the father's blindness to the doings of his sons, moreover since he is a teacher himself. I dare not communicate with him knowing his irrational dislike of me. This is why I write to you my dear Mrs. Barnett. Sincerely yours, Reverend Philip Cartney, B.A. H.Dip., President, Saint Martin's College, Lolinn.

MICHAEL: For the life of me I don't know how some of these fellows get into the Church, bloody refugees from the troubles of the world, hidden behind the smokescreen of Holy Orders.

SEAN: He writes a good letter.

MICHAEL: He has nothing better to do. (*Turns to Paddy*) What in the name of God has gotten into you? What are you? A shagging half-wit? What's this nonsense about epics?

PADDY: I started it three weeks ago.

MICHAEL: Don't you know you damned fool that all the good poetry has been written.

PADDY: An epic is different.

MICHAEL: What about your exam?

PADDY: That's not until June twelve months.

SEAN: What's an epic?

JACK: Some sort of long poem.

SEAN: Poetry is bad enough without having it long.

JACK: Still there should be some respect for it.

MICHAEL: What's this epic about? (*All gather round*).

PADDY: I'd rather not say.

MICHAEL: Please don't prevaricate with me. What's the theme?

PADDY: Alright. Picture a green field under a low-lying, cloudy sky. These clouds are wild and uncontrollable as they tumble across the great prairies of the heavens. They are charged with electricity with the result that you have an atmosphere of supercharged tension all around the field.

MICHAEL: The epic is about a field?

PADDY: No. It's about a football field and about a match which took place on it.

MICHAEL: What match?

PADDY: A challenge match.

MICHAEL: A challenge match between who?

PADDY: Between Ballybobee and Ballybobawn.

(*All laugh except Paddy*).

MICHAEL: Oh sweet Jesus that suffered for us. Tell me I'm hearing things.

LELUM: Ballybobee and Ballybobawn. Those teams are so bad that they're not even accepted in the junior league.

PADDY: Maybe not but they take their football seriously. It's like a religion with them.

MICHAEL: Those drunken bastards couldn't play football if they were paid. They're the biggest blackguards and the vilest thugs in the country.

PADDY: Only where football is concerned. You'll have to concede that.

MICHAEL: Granted. But what a subject for an epic. How many lines have you written?

PADDY: Nearly a thousand.

MICHAEL: Iambic pentameter naturally.

PADDY: Yes.

MICHAEL: How many more thousand do you propose to write?

PADDY: Oh . . . I should do it in twenty thousand lines all told.

MICHAEL: How long will it take you?

PADDY: A year and a half, maybe two years.

MICHAEL: And what about your exam?

PADDY: This is more important than any exam.

MICHAEL: I have news for you my friend. You will

abandon this epic at once and concentrate on your studies.

LELUM: You know when you come to think about it it's not a bad idea. The last time those two teams met in a football match the referee was all but murdered.

JACK: I remember that. The spectators fought for four hours after the game.

LELUM: Nineteen were taken to hospital including three women.

JACK: A man died a few months after as a result of a kick in the head.

PADDY: That's it. These teams are prepared to kill for football. They're prepared to die if needs be. That's why it has to be an epic. Can't you see it? The air of dreadful tension before the game, the supporters screaming for blood. The teams take the field. Suddenly the sky opens and old Mars himself, the great god of war, steps forth to start the game. He raises his hands aloft to the heavens and they respond with a fearful crack of thunder. That is the signal. The game is on and Ballybobee break away. The crowd goes berserk as the Ballybobawn backs absorb the first assault. The ball lands at midfield and Micky Donovan has it. He cuts through the Ballybobee defence like a scythe through switch grass. He takes a shot and the wind whips the ball aloft. It falls in the goal-mouth. There is a melee. Bots and fists fly. Blood flows free and men lie groaning in the square but the ball is in the net and it's a goal, a great goal for Ballybobee. The ball is placed for the kick-out . . .

MICHAEL: That will do.

PADDY: The ball is placed for the kick-out

MICHAEL: I said that will do. Enough of this infernal nonsense. Take your books and get into the house. (*Takes books and is about to depart*).

MICHAEL: And listen my friend . . . another single

solitary line of poetry of any kind during the school term and your mother won't know you when I'm done with you. I'm not finished yet. Yourself, Tom and you Lelum will join the defence forces forthwith. Discipline is what you all need and by God you're going to get it. Now get out of here before I forget we live in a civilised country.

(*Exit Paddy*)

LELUM: You're a notorious bluffer. Talking is not going to stop him. I know Paddy.

MICHAEL: I'll be the best judge of what's right for Paddy. (*To Jack and Sean*) Gentlemen I think it's time we had that drink.

JACK: (*Rubbing his hands together*) High time indeed. (*Extends courtesy of first exit to Sean*) After you Sean. Sail before steam. There will be no breach of maritime law while I'm aboard.

SEAN: So long Lelum.

LELUM: So long Sean.

(*Exit Sean*)

JACK: So long Lelum. I'll fix that job for Monday.

LELUM: Thanks Jack.

(*Exit Jack*)

MICHAEL: (*Indicates local security force band on his arm*). In a few days you'll be wearing one of these. You'll be serving your country at last.

(*Exit Michael*).

LELUM: I can't wait to see myself in uniform.

(*Curtain*).

ACT I SCENE III

Action as before. The time is the afternoon of a week later. The scene has changed slightly. Seated on the garden seat is Mary Barnett. Lelum wears the band of the local security forces on his arm. In the background are the upright shoreboards which will encase the wall.

Lelum is seen to be looking down into the aperture between the boards. He moves to where there is a mixture of cement and gravel and touches same with his shoe.

LELUM: If he doesn't come back soon this stuff will be gone hard. Where did he go anyway?

MARY: To the river for more gravel.

LELUM: What a wall this is going to be.

MARY: Come here Lelum and hold this yank of wool for me.

(He sits on seat and extends his hands. She entwines the yank round them and starts to make a ball of thread).

LELUM: I think he's using the wall to avoid reality.

MARY: I suppose in a way you're right but we're all the same aren't we? We all need something to hide behind at times. You and he don't seem to be hitting it off lately. I think you're under the impression he's failed you.

LELUM: Well hasn't he?

MARY: You mean because he didn't send you to the university?

LELUM: Among other things.

MARY: If you were an only son Lelum or if there were only two or even three of you the university would be no problem but there are four of you and then there are the girls. You don't know how lucky you are to have received a secondary education. When I was a girl only one in a thousand was so lucky.

LELUM: If he didn't drink so much.

MARY: He doesn't drink that much and when he does it's only in spasms. He works hard. Apart from the teaching there are the private tuitions. It's mostly the tuition money he drinks. He's never refused me anything. We don't know what hunger is. We have a fine home.

LELUM: I don't know what to do. I've no job.

29

MARY: You have your job in the bogs.

LELUM: We both know there's no future there. Anyway there's only another month of it.

MARY: You'll get a job and what's more you'll get a good job. You have brains Lelum and you're a good worker. You're young and strong and you're good looking. It's only a matter of time.

LELUM: I know what I'd really like to do but I'm almost afraid to say it.

MARY: You can say it to me. That's as far as 'twill go. Come on Lelum. You and I are too fond of each other to have secrets.

LELUM: Well . . . I'd like to become a professional actor . . . aren't you going to laugh?

MARY: Why would I laugh?

LELUM: Nobody from this town ever became a professional actor.

MARY: I should think that would be a reflection on the town.

LELUM: You mean you'd approve?

MARY: If it's what you really want Lelum I approve. I'll do all in my power to help you. Have you done anything about it?

LELUM: I've written here and there. I think I could get a scholarship to the National Theatre.

MARY: That would be marvellous.

LELUM What about himself?

MARY: You picked an unfortunate profession. He hates actors.

LELUM: I know. I've heard him.

MARY: According to him they're all idlers and seducers.

LELUM: There's more to it than that.

MARY: Of course there is. He once loaned five pounds to an actor. He was a member of a touring company. He never got it back. Then his first girl-friend was stolen from him by another actor who was also a member of a touring troupe.

LELUM: Better say nothing then.

30

MARY: Not for the present. You go ahead with your plans. We'll work it out. You know . . . I think you'd make a marvellous actor. There's something about you. I acted in a play once, the Colleen Bawn.

LELUM: I think the gravel-seekers are back.

MARY: Not a word about acting.

(*Enter Michael Barnett with a shovel on his shoulder. He is followed by Tom and Paddy wearing green armbands. Tom pushes a wheelbarrow full of gravel. He stops exhausted*).

TOM: (*To Paddy*) It's your turn. (*Tom flops on a seat*). (*Paddy pushes wheelbarrow across stage*).

PADDY: Where do you want it?

LELUM: Let me see now . . . I think you might leave it in the outhouse for the present.

(*Exit Paddy pushing barrow. At once Michael goes to the heap of gravel and cement and commences to mix it. He finds a bucket and goes to a water barrel. He returns to heap and pours some water on it. He mixes furiously with shovel, whistling happily*).

MARY: I think I'll go for a walk. I promised the girls I'd take them to the river. Are you coming Lelum?

LELUM: Yes I'll go with you.

MARY: Would you like a cup of tea Michael before I go?

MICHAEL: (*Without looking round*) No thanks. You go off and take the air. I can't afford to fall behind. That's why I must take advantage of every fine day.

MARY: Very well. We'll be off then. Don't overdo it Michael. Rome wasn't built in a day.

(*Exit Mary and Lelum*).

(*Michael continues to mix industriously. Seeing his opportunity Tom rises and tiptoes to exit. He is about to depart*).

MICHAEL: Where do you think you're going?

TOM: (*Surprised*) Nowhere. Nowhere at all.

MICHAEL: Get your books and start revising.

TOM: Now?

MICHAEL: Now.

(Tom locates books under table and selects a few. Enter Paddy).

PADDY: I left the wheelbarrow in the outhouse. I have to be off now. I'll see you all later. *(Heads for exit).*

MICHAEL: Come back here. Get out your books and get down to work.

(Reluctantly Paddy locates books under table and selects one at random. He sits near Tom. Michael shovels mixture into bucket and goes to wall).

MICHAEL: In future as well as night time studies there will be afternoon studies. *(They begin to expostulate).* I want no arguments. *(He pours bucket's contents into shored boards and locates a trowel with which he arranges mixture inside. He adds an adjacent stone or two).*

PADDY: I wonder what Homer's father said when he announced he was writing an epic?

TOM: He gave him every encouragement.

PADDY: Why do you say that?

TOM: Homer wrote the Odyssey didn't he? He wrote the Iliad. You don't write Odysseys and Iliads without help from your father. I can see old Homer senior patting the young fellow on the back and boasting about him to the neighbours . . . That's my son. He's the boy that writes the epics.

MICHAEL: Listen here you two, one more word and I'll send the pair of you to bed. How would you like that?

(The pair show exaggerated attention to the books).
(Enter Lily).

LILY: There's a man to see you master.

MICHAEL: What kind of man Lily?

LILY: He's not an insurance agent anyway master.

MICHAEL: How can you be sure?

LILY: Well he has a whisker master and a bag on his back.

32

MICHAEL: Then he can't be a process server either. Better send him on in Lily.

LILY: Yes master. (*Exit Lily*).

MICHAEL: Probably some poor devil with some sort of form to fill. (*More to himself*). Could be some relation of the wife's of course.

(*Enter a severely bearded man wearing an old hat and carrying a bag on his back. He would be in his late fifties or thereabouts. He is Moses McCoy*).

MOSES: (*To Michael*) Good day to you sir.

MICHAEL: Good day to you too sir. What can I do for you?

MOSES: Are you Barnett the schoolmaster?

MICHAEL: The very man. Come on in and take a seat. Would you like a cup of tea?

MOSES: (*Moving in*) No thank you master. I have here a drop of drink that does me more good than tea. (*He produces a bottle and takes a swig*).

MOSES: I suppose 'twould be no good asking you to have a drop of this master?

MICHAEL: I'm partial to all kinds of drink. What is it?

TOM: It smells like methylated spirits.

MICHAEL: In that case you'll forgive me if I decline. It's a beverage I don't care for. How can I help you?

MOSES: I have here a form to fill master.

MICHAEL: What kind of form?

MOSES: 'Tis for the claiming of money and property.

MICHAEL: British Army?

MOSES: Yes master. (*He produces bottle again*).

MICHAEL: That stuff will poison you. Put it away and we'll have a decent drink. (*To Tom*) Get a gollon from Lily and go down to Hogans for a half gallon of porter. Tell Hogan I'll square up at the end of the month.

(*Tom rises and makes for exit*).

MICHAEL: You tell Hogan it's for me personally, that I want pure porter, not slops or drippings. It must be direct from the wood and take none yourself. I'll

33

smell your breath when you come back just in case.

TOM: (*Digesting instructions*) A half gallon of pure porter . . . direct from the wood . . . drink none myself.

MICHAEL: Will you get along.

(*Exit Tom*)

MICHAEL: Have you got the form on you?

MOSES: Yes master. I have it here. (*He withdraws a crumbled form from his pocket. He hands it to Michael. Michael studies it carefully*).

MOSES: (*To Paddy*) What's he building there?

PADDY: It's a wall.

MOSES: For what?

PADDY: Privacy.

MOSES: Are you and the other chap his sons?

PADDY: That's right.

MOSES: I had sons once and I had a wife. She was a grand girl with red hair. She was tall too and slender like a willow. My sons were like giants. You never saw their likes.

PADDY: What happened?

MOSES: (*Points a finger upwards*) Mr. so-called God. (*Shakes fist upward*) Mister Blind God that one day I'll catch up with (*Insanely*) and strangulate and tear apart and crush to mincemeat. He'll answer to me when I meet him.

PADDY: Nearly everyone says God is good.

MOSES: Only people that lost nothing says that. God is not good and was never good. If he was good he wouldn't spend most of the time with his back turned, with his fingers in his ears and his eyes closed. God is cold and cruel. He gave us life alright but he gave us no means of keeping it. Don't talk to me about God.

MICHAEL: (*Looking up from form*) The total financial belongings of both boys amounts to thirty one pounds seven and three pence. Your full name is Moses McCoy?

MOSES: That is so master.

MICHAEL: (*Sits in place vacated by Tom. He writes on form*) What's your present address?

MOSES: I have none.

MICHAEL: I'll put you care of myself or some post office. Say which.

MOSES: Yourself master.

(*Michael writes on form*).

MICHAEL: Now . . . your wife's maiden name?

MOSES: Sheila Summertree.

MICHAEL: She will also have to sign this you know.

MOSES: She's dead.

MICHAEL: I'm sorry.

MOSES: It wasn't your fault. It was Mister so-and-so Bloody God.

MICHAEL: Bad enough losing your sons but your wife as well . . . is she long dead?

MOSES: She died the fourth of January eight years ago when there wasn't a leaf on a tree or a sign of sunlight. Consumption was the boy that took her but he was sent by God.

MICHAEL: Where did the boys die?

MOSES: El Alamein. The two together. A shell.

MICHAEL: Quite a few from around here were in the Eight Army. They all died. Some died at El Alamein. Others at Tobruk. They were little more than children when they left. What is your present occupation?

MOSES: You can put down I'm a wanderer.

MICHAEL: I can but it might hold up the money.

MOSES: I used to be a labouring man. Then the wife was taken. Then the boys. I sold the cottage and went through the money in a few months.   :

MICHAEL: Drink?

MOSES: What else? Marriage is a great thing master until the partner is taken.

MICHAEL: Marriage is the only true drama Moses. The moods, the conflicts, the love are paramount throughout. Unfortunately, like all great drama it must end

35

in tragedy when one of the principals bows out forever. I'll put down your occupation as labourer.
(*Writes*) What is your age?

MOSES: Fifty six.

MICHAEL: Your religion?

MOSES: (*Violently*) None.

MICHAEL: Into what religion were you born?

MOSES: I don't remember being baptised but I was
confirmed a Catholic.

MICHAEL: Catholic it is then. I think I have all I need
here. We'll have to have a witness of course. Sign
here Paddy.

(*Paddy accepts pen and signs*).

MICHAEL: Now Moses. If you will be good enough to
sign here.

(*Moses arrives at table*).

MICHAEL: As you will see the money amounts to thirty
one pounds seven shillings and three pence. Both
boys had watches, fountain pens and other odds and
ends. The watches were stolen but the other stuff
will be sent on. Write across here (*Hands him pen.
Moses signs*).

MOSES: Will I have long to wait?

MICHAEL: They're most efficient in the British War
Department. Not more than a week I would say. I'll
hold the letter for you.

MOSES: Do that master and we'll have a good long
drink.

(*Enter a flustered Lily in a hurry followed by Tom
bearing a gallon. Lily runs behind table while Tom
re-arranges hair and endeavours to look composed*).

MICHAEL: What's this about?

TOM: What's what about?

MICHAEL: Has he interfered with you in any way Lily?

LILY: No master. No.

MICHAEL: Are you sure?

LILY: Yes master. Yes, yes.

MICHAEL: Alright Lily. Bring a few glasses.

LILY: Yes master.

(Exit Lily)

MICHAEL: *(To Tom)* You sit down. *(Tom does so)* You're a man that's causing me great concern lately. So much so that I'll have to take serious steps to chastise you.

(Enter Lelum. He is followed by Lily bearing glasses. These she places on table and exits silently).

MICHAEL: *(To Lelum)* I thought you had gone to the river.

LELUM: Too many kids down there. I saw Tom coming out of Hogans with the gallon and I figured there might be some kind of celebration.

MICHAEL: If you were half as good at figuring out other things we'd all be the better of it.

LELUM: *(While Michael pours porter into three glasses).* Who is this?

PADDY: His name is Moses McCoy.

LELUM: How're you?

MOSES: Fine thank you.

(Michael hands a glass of porter to Moses who thanks him. He hands a glass to Lelum and takes a glass himself).

MICHAEL: I toast this wall which you see before you. May it stand when the names of Stalin and Hitler are erased from the memories of mankind.

(All Quaff)

MICHAEL: *(Replenishing glass which he has emptied at one swallow. To Tom)* There is something you had better know about women my friend.

(Lelum takes gallon and replenishes his own and Moses' glasses)

TOM: *(Keenly interested as is Paddy)* Yes dad.

MICHAEL: Any sort of extreme involvement with members of the opposite sex can be most dangerous, even fatal.

LELUM: Fatal?

MICHAEL: *(To Tom)* Remember that every time you

think about, talk to, kiss or caress a woman your heart beats at several times the normal speed. Now the heart has only so many beats and when these are exhausted there is that awful struggle for breath, that ultimate cry of anguish and despair and finally that last terrible gasp. (*Swallows porter and refills his glass. Lelum does likewise for himself and Moses*)

MICHAEL: (*To Tom*) If by merely thinking about women the heart beats faster imagine the speed if a man makes total love to a woman. It is not so bad for an old man as his heart is bigger and better developed but a young heart, say that of a man around the twenty mark, cannot possibly stand up to the strain of repeated strong courting and loving. He is wasting beats by the thousand and bringing on a sudden and untimely death. Every time you put your hands around a woman days, weeks, months are dropping from your life's span. It is my opinion Tom that unless you completely change your attitude towards the opposite sex you will die in your sleep one night very soon and then will come that awful day when your brothers and I will bear you from this house in a coffin and lay you to rest in a grave that is deep and dank and final. Maybe you think that is bad. That's only the beginning my friend for next will come the awful confrontation with your maker. He will ask you certain questions and when you have rendered an account for every single moment you spent on this earth he will pass sentence. Knowing you Tom and knowing of your past misdeeds there is only one place he can send you and Tom believe me when I say it is a spot where you'll see no angels and where you'll never be troubled with the cold. The next time you feel inclined to catch a hold of poor Lily think of that last awful encounter with your God.

MOSES: (*Jumps up suddenly and screams*) God is a cheat and a coward. God is a murderer. (*Challenging*

Stance) Come out God. Come out God wherever you are and face me like a man. Give me back the wife and sons you stole from me. (*Prances around Shadow boxing furiously*) Give me what's mine you cruelty man, you stinking, two-faced hypocrite that hides away whenever he's asked to relieve our misery. You're worse than the devil. It was you who created us. The devil never created anything except what you made for him. Come out I tell you 'till I see you. Come out you coward.

(*He flings empty glass against wall where it smashes*).

MICHAEL: My wall. My wall. What are you doing to my wall. In the name of God catch hold of him before he knocks what I've built.

(*Michael and Lelum seize him and aided by Tom and Paddy subdue him*).

MICHAEL: It's the bloody methylated spirits. Hold him down. Hold him.

PADDY: I think he's alright now. Are you alright now Moses?

(*Moses nods his head. He is seated on the ground flunked by Tom and Paddy. Lelum lets go of his hold of Moses' neck. Michael also releases hold on his legs*).

MICHAEL: He seems to be subdued. Why in God's name name did he fling the glass at the wall? Why not the table or the seat or the gable end of the house? Why not the outhouse? Why the wall?

LELUM: It could be a plot.

MICHAEL: A plot?

LELUM: Don't you see. Word of this wall has already spread far and wide. There's bound to be jealousy. There could be a conspiracy to sabotage it.

MICHAEL: Your particular brand of sarcasm will land you in serious trouble some day.

(*Paddy and Tom helps Moses to his feet*)

MOSES: I'm sorry master. I don't know what came over me.

(*Tom hands him his hat which fell off during the struggle*)

MOSES: When I think that I'll never see my wife or sons again I lose the head. Soon I'll put a finish to it all.

MICHAEL: Don't say that.

MOSES: My mind is made up. I've it planned a long time now.

MICHAEL: Time will straighten you out my friend.

MOSES: If I had the money from the War Department drank I'd go about it.

LELUM: Give the world a chance awhile yet. It's not as bad as you think.

MICHAEL: I think what we need is a drink. I don't feel like going back to the wall just yet. (*To Lelum*) Do you happen to have any money on you?

LELUM: I have five shillings.

MICHAEL: That's plenty. (*To Moses*) Bring your bag. You'll feel better after a pint of porter. (*To Tom and Paddy*) You two get back to work.

(*Exit Moses followed by Lelum and Michael*)

MICHAEL: (*Exiting — to pair who have just exited*) I always say there is no sanctum like a public house when pressures begin to mount.

(*To Paddy and Tom*) In precisely ten minutes take the wheelbarrow and bring a load of gravel from the river. Choose it well. I want no big stones and I want no mud. I want the stones to be small and of uniform size and I want the wheelbarrow full because when I come back I propose to make an all-out assault. Diversions such as we've experienced only serve to strengthen my resolve. Before the hot breath of August blows down the year that fragment of wall you see before you will stretch from there to there, rocklike and enduring, a finished work, in it's own right a masterpiece.

CURTAIN

SCENE 4

Action as before. This time in the afternoon of a week later. The wall has been extended a little although no great progress has been made. Michael Barnett is busily affixing scraps of plaster to that part of the wall which has been completed. Seated close by is his wife Mary. She is knitting a pullover.

MICHAEL: What do you think of it?

MARY: It's a bit early for comment yet.

MICHAEL: Still you must have some opinion.

MARY: It seems alright but then I'm no judge of walls.

MICHAEL: You think it's alright?

MARY: (*Putting aside knitting rises and examines wall from one end*). I hate to say this and I hate to have to be the one to tell you because no one else would dare but it seems a little bit crooked.

MICHAEL: Where?

MARY: (*Points*) There. In the middle and it seems to have sunk a bit here.

MICHAEL: Those faults are so minor that they are inconsequential. I more or less followed my instincts from the outset. If it is a shade crooked and if it has sunk a little that's all for the best. What it means is that the wall is merely following the natural contours of the place where it stands. It's a perfectly natural development. It's not perfect. None of us is. The idea from the beginning was the erection of a wall that would last. I never intended to build a show-piece. All I had in mind was a wall that would endure.

MARY: Of course. I wouldn't have said it at all but I thought you hadn't noticed.

MICHAEL: Of course I noticed.

MARY: Well . . . having said what I had to say I think it's going to be a fine wall.

MICHAEL: (*Standing back to admire his handiwork*) I think so too.

MARY: (*Returns and resumes her knitting*) I'm worried about the boys Michael.

MICHAEL: They're no different to any other boys of the same age.

MARY: Oh but they are. They're headstrong.

MICHAEL: What boy isn't?

MARY: They are at the age where it's difficult to talk to them and more difficult to handle them. If ever a boy deserved a hiding it was Tom. You left yourself down badly there.

MICHAEL: He hasn't been to the hayshed since.

MARY: How can you be sure?

MICHAEL: He promised me.

MARY: If you gave him the beating of his life when he deserved it there wouldn't be any need for promises and look at Paddy. We both know in our hearts that he's writing poetry non-stop.

MICHAEL: Deep down I feel that it's wrong to stop a boy from writing poetry. That's down deep. I realise of course that it will have to stop. I think it has and I think there's no need to say more. I know he dabbles away at it but dammit we don't want to kill his interest altogether.

MARY: You'll always find excuses. Then there's Lelum. He's anxious to get started in life, to make some sort of career for himself. You'd badly want to sit down and have a long talk with him.

MICHAEL: I think I might manage to send him to the university this coming October.

MARY: When did you change your mind?

MICHAEL: I've been thinking about it for some time and I think it can be done. It will mean giving up the drink but that might be no harm.

MARY: That's great entirely but the bother is he may not want to go to a university.

MICHAEL: Then what the hell does he want?

42

MARY: If you took the trouble to talk to him, to listen sympathetically, to encourage him to tell you about his hopes and his fears and his doubts but you won't do that.

MICHAEL: But beneath all the banter Lelum and I have a great love for each other. It's the same with the other two.

MARY: I know, but if they feared you more and respected you more it might be better for themselves. Sometimes instead of treating you like a father they treat you like a brother.

MICHAEL: What's wrong with that?

MARY: You are their father and it's your duty to drive them, to bully them, to forge them into men. You should be completely in command but you're not and they know you're not. When my brothers were their ages they dare not lift their voices, dare not contradict. They were afraid of their sacred lives of my father. Yet he hardly gave them three beatings in their lives but by God when he did it was years before they needed another. It was unpleasant and there was an atmosphere of horrible unrest in the house afterwards but signs on they are all well-adjusted, happy men today and to make men like that you must face up to the full responsibility of fathership no matter how unpleasant it may be. You must check up on your sons, spy on them if necessary for their own good. You must keep on their heels relentlessly if they are to grow up decently.

MICHAEL: I work hard with them. I'm always in touch.

MARY: In touch yes but never at grips. You won't look under the surface because you're afraid of what you'll see.

MICHAEL: You want me to be inquisitorial?

MARY: A father has the power and the right.

MICHAEL: If I look under the surface all I'll see is myself and all my weaknesses and that's not a pleasant sight. Essentially they're good boys. I love them and I am not going to dissect or analyse them. Let the world outside do that. That's what the world is for. You can only go so far with your children.

MARY: That sounds good but it's not the right way. Most of the other boys in the street . . .

MICHAEL: Most of the other boys in the street are being swept along with most of the other boys in the country. They have their standards and these standards do not allow them to think for themselves. It might jeopardise their exam chances or their jobs if they acted differently from the main herd. Jesus that would never do.

MARY: You want the boys to be different.

MICHAEL: Yes I do. I want them to be aware of things, not to be insensitive and unconcerned like ninety-nine per cent of mankind. I am not going to whip them along with the main herd.

MARY: They'll be stragglers then.

MICHAEL: They'll be observers and they'll see what the herd is really like and they'll be fortunate in that they'll see that there is a world outside the herd.

MARY: I'm no match for you.

MICHAEL: Oh yes you are when it suits you but on this occasion in your heart of hearts you agree with me.

MARY: In a sense but I don't want my sons to be freaks.

MICHAEL: They won't be. They'll feel. They'll record. They'll be conscious when others are deliberately unconscious.

MARY: Do you know that Tom never stops making passes at Lily?

MICHAEL: I don't think you need have any more worries on that score. I gave him a right talking to last week.

MARY: Well this happened last night.

MICHAEL: I can't believe it.

MARY: Lily is not the brightest you know. Also I have the feeling that he still goes to Hanratty's hayshed.

MICHAEL: But he can't, not since I nailed the front windows.

MARY: If he really want to go he'll go and nothing will stop him.

MICHAEL: I don't know what to say.

MARY: Say nothing. Just get your walking cane and make him so sore that he'll have something else to think about. Sometimes you make me sick. You close your eyes when there's a problem. Honestly there are times when I'm disgusted with you. You leave all the dirty work to me. I have to worry about the bills, about the future, about everything. When things get difficult you go and build a wall. That's your answer when your family really needs firm direction.

(*Enter Lily*)

LILY: Mister Trean and Mister Strong is outside sir.

MICHAEL: Send them right in Lily. (*Exit Lily*) (*Looks at his watch*) It's almost time for Haw-Haw.

MARY: You'll grasp at any straw rather than face up to your real responsibilities.

MICHAEL: Mary achree the world isn't worth all the attention you'd have me give it. Be satisfied that you and I are still in love. If the world had it's way we wouldn't be.

MARY: I suppose I'd better try and be content with my lot. There's no use arguing with you. You're beyond redemption.

(*Enter Jack Strong and Sean Trean. They exchange pleasantries with Mary*).

MARY: (*To all*) I have things to do.

SEAN: Don't say we're the cause of your going.

MARY: Indeed you're not Sean, I have to get the girls ready for bed. 'Bye all.

(*Exit Mary. Michael goes to wireless and turns knob. Almost at once there is a loud blast of martial brass. He modifies sound*).

MICHAEL: What's new?

SEAN: Father Barnum denounced Hanratty's hayshed

at devotions last night.

MICHAEL: You're not serious?

SEAN: From now on it's out of bounds for soldiers.

JACK: I don't know if that's wise. Soldiers have to have women.

SEAN: That's absolutely heinous.

JACK: What is?

SEAN: To make a vile charge like that against the Irish Army. They're not like the soldiers of other countries.

JACK: You mean they're not endowed with . . .

SEAN: I'm saying that this is a Catholic country.

MICHAEL: Easy now. It's on news time. (*He raises volume. Lelum enters*).

HAW-HAW: Station Bremen, Station Bremen. Germany calling, Germany calling. Good evening ladies and gentlemen and what a lovely evening it was in London until the sirens sounded the arrival of countless waves of German bombers. This bombing is a mere picnic compared to what the British can expect when the new German secret weapon descends like an avenging angel from the heavens. Against it there can be no defence.

(Enter Paddy and Tom bearing strapped parcels of books. They gather round).

HAW-HAW: The recent British announcement that all German resistance in North Africa has ended is causing genuine and prolonged laughter to the German people. The withdrawal of all German forces from the worthless deserts of the Dark Continent is merely part of the great counter offensive against Russia.

SEAN: Hear, hear. (*Claps his hands*).

HAW-HAW: Our Panzer divisions are re-grouping and soon these inexorable units aided by a new terrible weapon will ring the death knell for the Allies. The cities of Britain wil be bombed out of existence.

SEAN: Proper bloody order.

MICHAEL: Silence sir.

HAW-HAW: Consequently the British announcement that all German resistance in North Africa is crushed can be seen as another fairy tale. It is the wish of the Fuehrer that the real war now commence on the East European Front where twenty Panzer divisions will annihilate the starving armies of Russia.

MICHAEL: Turn it off. (*Tom does so at once*).

LELUM: I wonder if they've really got a secret weapon.

SEAN: You can be sure of it.

JACK: Every Irish soldier has the same secret weapon, only waiting for the chance to use it.

SEAN: You mock the tradition of the Fianna who revered and venerated the purity of Irish womanhood . . . You belittle the noble heritage of the Irish fighting man.

MICHAEL: Now . . . now . . . now. (*He proceeds to mix cement and gravel*) Let there be no more arguing. (*To Paddy and Tom*) You two go in and have your supper. Then straight to your books.

JACK: (*To Tom*) Did you hear Hanratty's hayshed was denounced from the pulpit?

TOM: I know nothing about that place. I never go near it now.

JACK: It's been put out of bounds to soldiers and it's to be locked and barricaded from now on.

TOM: That has nothing to do with me.

LELUM: Of course not. Everybody knows that. (*Mockery to Jack*) How dare you suggest that this man would demean himself by visiting such a place.

TOM: (*To Lelum*) Watch it.

LELUM: You're the one that should watch it.

TOM: What are you trying to say?

LELUM: (*Meaningfully*) I said you are the one that should watch it, not me.

TOM: It would help if you clarified.

LELUM: Would it? I know more about you than you think.

PADDY: (*Urgently*) Cut it out. (*To Sean*) You were saying Sean.

SEAN: Our Irish virgins would never debase themselves. Our soldiers come from decent homes where the fear of God and love of Ireland go hand in hand.

JACK: Well let me tell you something Sean Trean. Your Irish boys and girls are no angels. Did you know Hanratty's mule died yesterday?

SEAN: What has Hanratty's mule to do with it?

SEAN: Did you hear Michael?

MICHAEL: (*Absorbed with shovelling mixture into bucket*). I have no time to be involved in argument just now. Carry on without me. Nothing in this world and I mean nothing is going to stay the building of this wall between here and nightfall. (*Takes full bucket to shored boards and empties it therein. Busies himself with trowel arranging it inside*).

PADDY: I heard about the mule. He collapsed going to the creamery or something.

JACK: Or something is right. I'll tell you how he died. Until recently that mule was a healthy five year old without a blemish, as fine an animal as was ever fathered by a stallion ass. Yet suddenly he collapses. Mrs. Hanratty suspected he might be poisoned so she sent for Dick Savage the vet. Dick Savage opened the mule's belly, right down the middle. (*To Sean*) You know what he found?

SEAN: How the devil do I know?

JACK: I'm asking you what Dick Savage the vet found in the stomach of Hanratty's mule?

SEAN: You tell me.

JACK: I'll tell you alright. He found one partly-digested, outsize ladies' corset which no doubt once restrained the bulging belly of one of your famous Irish virgins.

SEAN: Rubbish.

JACK: Ask the vet. He found two brassieres also partly digested. He found three ladies slips very well chewed, one of 'em embroidered. He found what

48

looked like the remnants of eleven silk stockings and a buckle from a woman's shoe. He found the partial remains of eleven pairs of ladies' knickers, thoroughly ground up and all but digested and last but not least twenty seven pairs of ladies' home-made elastic garters. Now are you convinced that your Irish soldier is no different from any other soldier?

LELUM: If the knickers and the corsets were partly digested and presumably on their way to being fully digested what was the actual cause of death?

PADDY: I know. 'Twas the buckle.

JACK: No it wasn't It was the garters. The mule was unable to digest the elastic.

SEAN: I don't believe one word of it. Ladies' knickers indeed.

JACK: All you have to do is ask the vet if you don't believe me. What surprises me is that the unfortunate mule found knickers there at all because half those ones coming into town now never wore knickers in their lives.

SEAN: (*Explodes*) These are heinous and unfounded allegations.

JACK: Half of them wouldn't know a pair of knickers from a pair of polo drawers.

MICHAEL: (*Suddenly turning from his labours to Paddy and Tom*) In the name of God have you two gone in yet?

TOM: We were just leaving.

MICHAEL: Get out of it and get straight to your books the minute you've eaten.

PADDY: How's the wall going dad?

MICHAEL: You might say it's at the critical stage. That's why I have to devote all my powers of concentration to it. For that reason I will repeat myself for the last time and ask the two of you to get indoors and have your supper.

49

TOM: It seems to me to be a bit crooked here and look here. It seems to have sunk.

MICHAEL: Those are small things, easily rectified. The main object is to get the thing built. It will be an easy matter to polish it up when it's finished. Now for the final time get in to your supper.

TOM: Just trying to offer a bit of helpful criticism.

MICHAEL: (*Shouts*) I'll count three and if the two of you have not gone indoors by that time . . . one . . . two . . .

(*Exit Paddy and Tom*)

MICHAEL: It's easy to criticise. It's not so easy to create.

JACK: We called to find out if you were coming for a gargle?

MICHAEL: To tell you the truth boys I'm a bit low in the pocket. Payday is still a week to go.

JACK: Come on. I have enough for the three of us.

MICHAEL: No thanks. That's not my way.

LELUM: Your word is good at Hogans.

MICHAEL: I'm already up to my eyes at Hogans. Anyway, I've made up my mind that nothing is going to come between me and this wall, not for the next few days at any rate. You two go ahead . . .

LELUM: I see your friend Moses McCoy approaching. (*Points towards outhouse*).

(*Jack and Sean join Lelum*).

JACK: He's the fellow who drinks the meths.

SEAN: Talks to himself.

JACK: Offers God out to fight.

MICHAEL: He's a simple man who lost his wife and family. He won't resign himself to the loss and that's probably because he's not able.

(*Enter Moses McCoy*).

MOSES: Good evening master. (*To others*) Good morrow to you men.

MICHAEL: Good evening to you Moses.

MOSES: Have you had any account from the War Department master?

50

MICHAEL: The letter came yesterday Moses. Hang on there a minute and I'll get it for you.
(*Exit Michael. Moses examines the wall. He is watched carefully by Jack and Sean*).

LELUM: What do you think of it?

MOSES: Who am I to criticise the work of a schoolmaster?

LELUM: This is Jack Strong and this is Sean Trean. This is Moses McCoy boys.
(*They acknowledge each other*).

LELUM: It's a nice evening thanks be to God.

MOSES: Why should you thank God for an ordinary evening? If God wanted to he could make every evening beautiful and every day too and every night. There would be no man cold and there would be no man wet but God don't want to do that. All God wants is for people to suffer, people who does him no harm.

LELUM: God isn't so bad.

MOSES: You won't say that when you're my age, that's if you live to be my age. God might get a mad fit and carry you off.

SEAN: All the same we should be thankful to be alive.

MOSES: Why should be? We didn't ask to be born. I didn't give God permission to bring me into this place of torture. It's a good thing I don't need his permission to get out.

LELUM: Don't talk like that Moses.

MOSES: God don't consult with me. I'm the man that knows what's best for me. All I ever wanted was to be with my wife and to see my sons settled down. God interfered without my permission. Could you beat it. Without a word he stole all I loved and left me alone. Is he such a fool that he thinks I'm going to stay here when my wife and sons is with him? If he won't come to me soon and render account then

I'll go to him. One quick dart across here (*indicates throat*) and I'll be face to face with him.

(*Instinctively Jack and Sean cover their throats*).

(*Enter Michael*).

MICHAEL: (*Holding letter aloft*) Here it is Moses. (*He hands it to Moses who rips it open. He extracts cheque and flings envelope away*).

MOSES: Thirty one pounds seven shillings and threepence. This is the price paid by the wretch we call God for my two sons. Thirty one pounds seven shillings and threepence. Hardly sixteen pounds apiece. Who says thank God now? What fool says God is good? God is no damned good, never was and never will be world without end . . .

MICHAEL: Now, now, Moses. Don't upset yourself. (*Places a hand on his shoulder*).

MOSES: I'd like to give you a few pounds for your trouble master.

MICHAEL: You owe me nothing.

MOSES: A drink then. We'll have a good drink, all of us.

MICHAEL: You couldn't have asked me at a worse time. I'm up to my neck in this wall . . .

MOSES: Don't renege on me master. There's enough reneged on me.

MICHAEL: Well I'll have one then.

LELUM: If you'll have one you'll have two.

MICHAEL: I can't refuse the man. Anyway he'll need somebody to identify him if he wants the cheque cashed.

MOSES: Come on all. We'll have a night of it. No one pays but me. All friends of the master are friends of mine. Come on now. I won't hear of no . . .

(*He leads Michael off. They are followed by Sean. Exit all three. Jack Strong is about to exit but sees that Lelum is not leaving*).

JACK: What's the matter? Aren't you coming?

LELUM: One drunkard in the house is enough.

JACK: I know you don't mean that.

LELUM: I mean it. There's no future for me here.

JACK: You'll feel better after a drink. Come on now . . . (*Pushes him towards exit*). *Exit Lelum*.

JACK: I told him. I said you build a wall and you give everybody else a licence to do the same. Look what's happened. Mr. Moses McCoy has built a wall between himself and God. Hanratty's hayshed is out of bounds to lovers and now Lelum is starting to build a wall of his own. (*Shakes his head*) Believe me there will be many an up and down before this damned wall is finished.

CURTAIN

ACT 2

Action as before. The time is three weeks later. It is well into July. A fine starry night. Michael Barnett is busily re-arranging cement and gravel mixture within shored boards. The wall has reached the half way stage. At one side Moses McCoy uses a shovel to mix cement and gravel. From time to time he adds a little water.

MOSES: How long now since you started it master?

MICHAEL: Let me see. (*Cogitates*) It must be five or six weeks all told. God knows I suppose it could be the six weeks. Of course I could do nothing for the past fortnight between the rain and storm.

MOSES: That's the truth. Only for the break in the weather you'd have it finished by now. There's no sane man would deny that.

MICHAEL: Still you'll have to admit that the critical stage is past. It should be all plain sailing from now on. Let's have a drop of porter before we proceed any further.

(*He goes to table and pours from enamel bucket into glasses*).

MOSES: I see your soldier son at home master.

MICHAEL: He is. He is. He got a week's leave. Unfortunately he goes back tomorrow.

MOSES: He's a fine man for his years.

MICHAEL: He's all that. Isn't he a grand sight in the uniform?

MOSES: Oh without doubt.

MICHAEL: Of course I had an uncle as fine a man as ever broke bread. In fact my father and grandfather were exceptional fellows. They had a great natural strength.

MOSES: You're no bad man yourself master.

MICHAEL: One time Moses. One time.

MOSES: I had great sons master. The two of them were well over the six feet and as broad as that wall you're building. The strength of them would frighten you . . . and to be carried away by that hobo that scoffs at us all above in his heaven. My wife, master, was a beauty. I often wished she was eighty years of age so I wouldn't be jealous of her anymore. (*Points upwards*) You see all them stars . . . all them together wasn't as bright as her smile. Her hair was red but sometimes when the wind played on it 'twould turn to russet or if 'twas caught in the light of the sun 'twould take a hundred shades. one of 'em brighter than the next. Oh Jesus master 'twas an awful sweeping. If I had God now I'd break him in two. I'll face him soon though and then he'll have nowhere to hide from me . . . (*Produces bottle of methylated with which he laces porter. He proffers bottle to Michael who recoils*). ·

MICHAEL : You'll face God quicker than you think if you keep drinking that stuff. Why don't you drink whiskey itself?

MOSES : My money is all gone master.

MICHAEL : Considering everything it made a fair battle. Good health to you Moses. (*He quaffs from his glass*).

MOSES : I notice master you seldom drink spirits of any kind.

MICHAEL : It's not by choice I assure you. It agrees neither with my constitution nor my pocket. There are times when I become ravenous for it. I love whiskey. I love the gurgle of it in the snout of a bottle and I love the rich plop of it when it falls into a glass. I love the way it babbles and bubbles when a bottle is shaken. As for the taste of it I find it goes beyond words. That first drop of it hits the walls of the chest a ferocious rattle but after that it lights up the interior and there is a wonderful lunacy in the head. Ah Moses there were few born with the natural love of whiskey that was granted to me. (*Enter Mary Barnett. She is followed by Lily*).

MARY: I want to speak to you Michael. Something very serious has happened.

MICHAEL: Yes Mary. What is it?

MARY: I'm afraid it's private Michael.

MICHAEL: Well I can't right away. It's a dry night and that heap of cement mix over there is likely to get hard unless I use it up at once.

MARY: It's important.

MICHAEL: I know. I won't be long dear.

MARY: I have a few things to do I won't press you now. I'll be back in ten minutes and I want nobody here but members of our own family. Come along Lily.

(*Exit Mary Barnett followed by Lily. Michael stands puzzled, wondering*).

MOSES: I'll go.

MICHAEL: No. She didn't mean it like that.

MOSES: She's like a woman who would have enough of outsiders in the place for a while.

MICHAEL: You think so?

MOSES: I call on many a house master and I can tell a woman's moods.

MICHAEL: That's more than I can do. Fill me a bucket of the mixture. (*Moses goes to the stuff he has been mixing and Michael returns to the wall*).

MICHAEL: You know this wall is a good exercise in discipline. What I mean is that there can be no relaxation. Nothing worthwhile was ever accomplished haphazardly. You see a monument to a dead hero or a great bridge spanning a deep gorge. It was not the laying of stone upon stone that made these buildings noteworthy. Any fool could do that. No my friend it was the everlasting attention to the small details.

(*He drops a few adjacent stones into the wall and arranges them inside the shored boards*).

MOSES: I couldn't build a wall, at least not on my own. Maybe if I was shown I could make a fair attempt.

56

I'd want someone looking over my shoulder all the time or if I had a wall drawn out for me on a blackboard that I could copy . . .

MICHAEL: I know what you mean. At the outset you must have a concept. You must be able to see the completed product clearly in the mind's eye. There can be no carelessness, no reckless slapping together of stone and cement. There has to be a plot like there is in a play.

(*Moses arrives at wall with bucket of mixture which he hands to Michael*).

MICHAEL: I must say that this is well mixed. You mixed concrete before this I would say.

MOSES: I tended a mason for a year and I tended a plasterer for another.

MICHAEL: I knew you were no novice. (*He pours mixture into shored boards. With a trowel he re-arranges it. He locates a sledge and stomps the heavy head of it on the insides of the boards. Moses busily mixes and then fills bucket with shovel*).

MICHAEL: We make a good team Moses.

MOSES: I'm only a labourer master. Any man could do what I do but only a man in a hundred has the ability to build a wall.

(*Moses arrives at wall and hands bucket to Michael. Michael pours contents into shored boards and returns bucket to Moses who returns to mix another bucketful*).

(*Enter Mary Barnett*).

MARY: Have you time to talk to me now?

MICHAEL: Out of the question. We're up to our eyes. See for yourself. When that mix is used up I'll devote the whole night to you.

MARY: Alright. I'll give it one more try. You keep to your wall just yet but when I return to this place in fifteen minutes you will have to choose between me and the wall.

(*Exit Mary*).

MICHAEL: I don't know what's coming over the woman.

MOSES: The best thing is to talk to her and find out.

MICHAEL: I will. I will as soon as I finish here.

MOSES: She seems a very agitated woman. I have the feeling I should start evacuating. Women are like the ocean, peaceful and calm one minute and the next violent and raging. That woman is simmering with a bit. I'd say she's near the boil.

MICHAEL: I wouldn't worry. The important thing is that this wall goes well. At no stage since I began it did I make such headway. A few more days and nights of this and we'll have a wall of our own.
(*Enter Jack Strong and Sean Trean. They wear their armbands*).

SEAN: (*To Jack*) And I say to you that Ireland divided will never be at peace.

MICHAEL: (*To Moses*) Can you imagine it in the Autumn covered with lichens and draped with red ivy. Picture it in your mind. The wind rustles through the ivy and a flight of starlings suddenly erupts from the depths with a whirring of tiny wings. Or picture it in the moonlight when the beams of silver fall on the ivy leaves. What a romantic place this back garden will be when that day comes. (*Noticing Sean Trean and Jack Strong for the first time*) Ah gentlemen . . . What do you two think now?

JACK: You've really made progress. I can't believe it.

SEAN: There's no doubt but you've passed the critical stage.

JACK: If the weather holds and it looks like it will it wouldn't surprise me if the wall wasn't standing on it's own two feet by the end of July.

MICHAEL: I agree with you but I am not going to make the fatal mistake of setting myself a time limit. I am not going to be rushed. That could mean mistakes and I can't afford to make one at this stage.
(*Sean Trean examines the enamel bucket*).

58

MICHAEL: I'm afraid it's empty Sean. Building is dry work.

SEAN: We had a notion of going to Hogans for a few.

MICHAEL: Don't let me stop you.

JACK: Aren't you coming?

MICHAEL: How can I? Conditions are ideal for building and anyway the missus wants a word with me. Maybe later.

(*Enter Lelum followed by Paddy and Tom. Tom would seem to have a black eye. He carries togs and football boots and jersey wrapped up in a bundle. Paddy wears togs, stockings and football boots. He carries his clothes in an untidy bundle*).

SEAN: Who won the match?

LELUM: 'Twas never finished. The bloody crowd rushed the pitch.

MICHAEL: (*Advances*) Were the three of you stuck in the row?

LELUM: We were lucky we weren't kicked to death. We ran for it.

MICHAEL: (*To Tom*) What happened to you?

TOM: I ran into somebody's fist.

MICHAEL: (*To Tom and Paddy*) Get inside and change and come right back here for further instructions.

TOM: There's a dance on tonight. The exam is over.

MICHAEL: I said report right back here for instructions.

TOM: (*Saluting stiffly*) Yessir.

(*Exit Tom and Paddy*).

MICHAEL: Where's Tony?

LELUM: He's bringing on the girls.

MICHAEL: Who started the fight?

LELUM: Somebody booed a decision by the referee and the crowd ran on to the field.

JACK: That would never happen in rugby. There's no discipline in Gaelic Football. A young lad could be maimed and he could whistle for justice.

SEAN: You never liked our native games.

JACK: That's not so. What I'm saying is that there isn't enough discipline.

SEAN: And what I'm saying is that any Irishman who plays rugby is a swine.

JACK: Will you listen to that!

SEAN: And any Irishman who watches the game of rugby is a bigger swine. He is a low-down, dirty, stinking sewer rat. You can take your British garrison games and you can stick them up in the highest rafter of you know where.

JACK: What chance has this country when we have mentalities like this? There will never be an end to stupidity.

SEAN: There will never be an end to the Gaelic tradition, to the ideal that Ireland is the proudest nation in Europe, the oldest nation in Europe and according to the Pope the most Catholic country of all. I'll spell it out once more. Any Irishman who plays soccer, rugby or cricket is a dirty renegade.

MICHAEL: What about pitch and toss?

SEAN: It's not as bad as the games I've mentioned.

JACK: What about ju jitsu?

MICHAEL: And Russian roulette?

MOSES: And toodleumbuck . . . the more you put down the less you take up.

SEAN: Mocking is catching.

MICHAEL: And it's not going to get this wall built. (*Enter Tony Barnett, the oldest son. He is dressed in the uniform of the Irish Army. He wears a field cap and the lanyard of the artillery*).

SEAN: Ah Tony . . . and how are you enjoying your holiday? (*Places his arm around Tony's shoulder*).

TONY: Great entirely Sean.

JACK: What was the match like?

TONY: It was alright 'till the spectators joined in.

JACK: Ah yes. The great Gaels of Ireland.

SEAN: (*To Jack*) Can you think of nothing good to say about your native land?

JACK: I can but it wouldn't be good enough for you. (*To Tony*) So you're away tomorrow.

TONY: Yes Jack. I'll have to be in the barracks at ten o'clock tomorrow night.

SEAN: Duty first. When duty calls a soldier must obey. (*Enter Paddy and Tom. They wear armbands. They are followed by Lelum*).

TOM: Reporting for further instructions.

TONY: I see you're all in the Local Security Force.

MICHAEL: All except Moses.

SEAN: Now that we have a professional soldier in our midst why shouldn't we let him put us through our paces. (*All gather round Tony eagerly*).

TONY: I'm not a drill master. I'm just a private soldier who's never given an order in his life.

MICHAEL: You're a trained soldier and that's all that matters. Come on lads. Get your weapons.
(*They all make haste to find whatever mock rifles they can. Moses and Michael use shovels, Sean Trean uses a sledge. Others locate convenient pieces of timber*).

TONY: Ah come off it. I'm no use at this kind of jazz.

MICHAEL: You'll do. You're good enough for us.

SEAN: This is a great moment for the town of Lolinn. Imagine to be drilled by a man I knew as a child, a man I helped to rear.

MICHAEL: Line up there now. We want no farcing. This has to be serious. Let's find out how good we are.

SEAN: It may not be much in the eyes of the outside world but for us this is a highly historical occasion. (*They make an uneven line across the stage*).

JACK: (*To Lelum*) What a pity we haven't a camera. The world shouldn't be deprived of a sight like this. (*When they are lined up they await instructions eagerly. They hold their rifles at various angles, all different*).

MICHAEL: We're waiting Tony.

TONY: Oh, well — Gasra aire.

(They all come to attention, except Moses).

Ardíg Arum.

(They shoulder arms. Business — Sean puts 'rifle' on wrong shoulder. Jack takes pleasure in correcting him).

Déanaighe dhá líne.

(They form a double line. Business — Jack swings Moses round).

Clé casaígh.

(They turn to left, except Sean).

SEAN: *(aside to Jack)* In the name a' Jazus what's "cosseage"?

JACK: Left turn!

SEAN: *(Turns)* Oh!

TONY: Go mear máirséal. *(All march off whistling).*

(Alone on stage Tony shakes his head with a smile. He goes to wall and examines latest developments there. Off can be heard the distant sound of whistling. The volume increases and the company enters whistling the boys of Wexford or the likes. They march across stage and exit at the other side. While they are off Mary Barnett enters).

MARY: *(Shakes her head)* God help us all. They've no more sense than children.

TONY: *(Immediately concerned by her air of worry)* What's the matter mother?

MARY: Does it show that much Tony?

TONY: You look down and out. Is anything wrong?

MARY: There's a lot wrong Tony.

TONY: Can you tell me?

MARY: I wouldn't know where to begin. Wait 'till your father and the boys come back and the rest have gone. There's a lot to be said. It's not for outsiders to hear. This can only be resolved by ourselves. I could cry my eyes out this minute if it would do any good.

TONY: Ah come on now mother. It can't be that bad.

62

MARY: It's bad enough Tony. Tony I want you to tell me something.

TONY: If I can.

MARY: About girls Tony.

TONY: What about them?

MARY: Do you respect them?

TONY: Yes . . . of course.

MARY: You go out with girls a lot?

TONY: Some week-ends yes.

MARY: Are you going steady?

TONY: Oh mother, on twenty one shillings a week?

MARY: But do you have a regular girl?

TONY: Why don't you tell me what you really want to know and I'll do my best to answer?

MARY: Alright. Do you respect all the girls you go with?

TONY: I don't fully understand you.

MARY: I just want to know if you behave yourself with girls?

TONY: I don't know how to answer that one. I don't know exactly what you mean by behave.

MARY: You kiss girls.

TONY: Of course.

MARY: Do you go beyond that?

TONY: I don't know what you're driving at.

MARY: Oh don't be so evasive Tony. Will you please tell me if you've ever been familiar with a girl?

TONY: (*Seeking an avenue of escape*) Familiar . . . What's that supposed to mean?

MARY: Jesus Tony have you ever been intimate with a girl?

TONY: Look mother I don't know what to say to you. I love you and respect you and I don't want to disillusion you. The army is a hard school. There are different codes. I go out with girls because I'm lonely. These girls are not like the girls in the street here. They've been thrown out in the world. They have different attitudes.

63

MARY: Thank you Tony. I think you've answered my question although I would have thought more of you if you had told me at once.

TONY: Oh mother don't make it so hard for me. I feel rotten. (*He goes to her and places his hands on her shoulders and looks into her face*).

TONY: Of course I've been intimate with women. There's a world war going on around us and I'm a soldier. I have never wronged a girl or I've never misled an innocent girl. I know I've done terrible wrong by your standards but my own I'm not so bad. What's happened to me has happened to every mother's son. I want you to know mother that I respect girls whether they expect it or not. I know you're disillusioned with me.

MARY: Disillusioned is it. There's no word for what I feel just now.

TONY: (*Torn*) What can I do or say to get you to understand?

MARY: It's alright Tony.

TONY: Don't be angry with me.

MARY: I'm not. It's just that I took certain things for granted. I'm hurt and I'm disappointed but I'm not angry with you Tony. Understand that.

TONY: Yes mother.

MARY: I keep forgetting you're not my baby anymore, that you're a man of the world, that you have to be what you are.

(*Tony turns his head aside. She would go to him to console him but she hesitates. Then from a distance can be heard the beat of a drum and different but uniform whistling. The volume increases. Enter the company. At the rear Paddy beats on a toy drum, it is ancient and battered but effective, nonetheless. The company is deadly serious and intent on presenting a military appearance. They pass by and exit but not before Mary Barnett seizes Tom and pulls him aside. The others ignore everything. Exit the company*).

TOM: (*Airily*) I was enjoying it. What's the matter anyway?

MARY: Don't you know?

TOM: Know what?

MARY: About Lily?

TOM: What about Lily?

MARY: I'm deadly serious Tom so don't play about with me. You mean you don't know what's the matter with Lily?

TOM: Cross my heart I don't know what you're talking about. Honestly mother I don't. (*Turns to Tony*). What is it anyway? What's all this jazz about Lily.

TONY: I don't know.

MARY: I'm weak with the worry that's on top of me this day. Tom had you anything to do with Lily since she came to work for us?

TOM: What are you on about?

MARY: Answer the question.

TOM: I would if I knew what you meant.
(*Mary suddenly snatches stick from his hand and lets him have it heavily across the body*).

TOM: (*Jumps backward*) Hey look-out, that hurts.

MARY: You don't know what hurt is Tom. Poor Lily O'Dea knows what hurt is. Poor innocent Lily O'Dea that I thought was safe under my roof.

TOM: (*Not convincing. To Tony*) Somebody tell me what it's all about.

MARY: You know what it's all about.

TOM: But I don't.

MARY: Don't you know she's going to have a baby?

TOM: What?

MARY: A baby. You know what a baby is?

TOM: Yes. I do.

MARY: Well Lily is going to have one of them. Come nearer to me Tom. (*He draws near to her*) Do you know anything about this baby?

65

TOM: What would I know?

(*Suddenly Mary unleashes a vicious swipe with stick and catches him fairly with it. He covers his head with his hands but makes no attempt to evade the second swipe*).

MARY: (*Loudly*) What would you know Tom. Is that what you say . . . You're a hard one Tom, a hard man. I never dreamed I would rear a son like you. If I knew in time I wouldn't have bothered. I'd have taken my breast away from you and let you wither. (*She strikes him viciously across the legs*) Now will you tell me about Lily O'Dea?

TOM: It was only once. I swear it was only once. They were all doing it to her, all the lads.

MARY: No they weren't. Lelum wasn't and Paddy wasn't. You were the one. The poor girl was in our charge, in our care. She was entrusted to us. What in the name of Mary am I going to tell her mother. What am I going to say to her? How am I going to begin. A son of mine is the father of the bastard your daughter is going to have. My son Tom is the man.

TOM: Mother, mother listen to me. It's not true. She had soldiers long before me. She had other fellows, farmers boys and clerks long before me. I swear that to you mother. I'm not responsible.

MARY: Will you listen to him.

TOM: (*Advancing with his hands outstretched*) As true as God mother!

MARY: The poor fooleen of a girl. She named them all, all the soldiers, all the others. She didn't name you Tom. She wouldn't tell me about you because you were of the house. Innocent as she is she knew what you did was the worst. You betrayed a trust. You cheated on your upbringing and the faith she had in you. I had to ask her. I had to be sure. I wouldn't be a good mother if I didn't make certain.

(*Tony advances towards her but she wards him off*).

TONY: Mother you're being too hard on yourself.

MARY: I had to be satisfied. Were there any others? I asked. She didn't answer. Tell me the truth Lily I said. She still wouldn't answer me. Was Tom one of them I asked. No answer. Was Tom one of them I asked again. This time she nodded her head and she cried her eyes out.

TOM: It was only a few weeks ago I was with her. I had nothing to do with the child. That happened long before.

MARY: Maybe so but what matters is that you took advantage of her and which is worse you did it under this roof. I never thought I'd live to see the day that a son of mine would dishonour an innocent. You . . . (*She beats him relentlessly across the garden*) You vile and wretched thing. At this moment I wouldn't care if I never saw you again in my life . . . (*He falls in a heap at one side*).

MARY: I don't deserve it from him.

TONY: No you don't but you're too hard on yourself. You should be more prepared for this sort of thing.

MARY: More prepared? Don't you ever say a thing like that again. How could any mother be prepared for what he did?

(*Tony helps Tom to his feet and thence to a chair. He sits hangdog. In the distance can be heard the whistling and the drum. This time the tune is 'It's a Long Way to Tipperary'*).

MARY: Will they ever grow up?

TONY: They're happy and at least that something.

MARY: You haven't had much of a holiday Tony. I'm sorry but I wouldn't be much of a mother to either one of you if I closed my eyes to reality. I was tempted to do it, tempted to pretend that Tom was innocent.

(*The whistling and druming grows louder*).

MARY: Bring them to a halt this time Tony like a good boy.

TONY: Whatever you say.

(*Enter the company, as game and as martial as ever, proudly swinging along, heads held high, whistling their hearts out*).

TONY: Greadáig fúibh.

(*They mark time*).

Gasra stad.

(*They halt*).

Clé casaíg).

(*They turn left*).

Gaonáig airm.

(*They bring arms to side*).

Seasaíg araís.

(*They stand at ease*).

Gasra scaipíg.

(*They dismiss*).

MICHAEL: As fine a body of men begobs as you'd find anywhere.

SEAN: True for you. What do you think Tony?

TONY: There's no doubt but you're as good as any I've seen.

SEAN: We're ready and we're waiting. We won't be found wanting when the hour comes.

JACK: What hour?

SEAN: The hour our country needs us.

JACK: The day the country depends on the likes of us that's curtains for the country.

MICHAEL: Now, now. Don't be too sure. (*He immediately proceeds to where mixture is and commences to mix with shovel*) Remember Thermopylae? They were only a handful.

MARY: I'd like a talk with you Michael.

MICHAEL: Later Mary . . . later.

MARY: Sorry Michael. This can't wait. It will have to be now.

MICHAEL: (*Filling bucket*) Alright but you'll have to hang on 'till I unload this bucket. (*Takes bucket and pours contents into shored boards. Is about to rearrange with trowel when Mary advances*).

MARY: For the last time Michael.

MICHAEL: Very well . . . (*To Sean and Jack*) I think I'll go to Hogans with you after all. I could do with a few pints. God knows it's been a long day. Hang on there just awhile lads 'till I listen to my long-suffering wife. Now Mary girl what is it?

MARY: It's for the family.

MICHAEL: You know Sean and Jack. There's no need for . . .

MARY: Listen to me Michael and get it through your head. I don't want Jack and Sean to hear what I have to say.

JACK: We were just going anyway.

MICHAEL: It must be something terrible altogether . . . (*Jack and Sean hang on although they have edged towards exit*).

MARY: In the name of God will you tell them to go. What do you want them for anyway? What good are they to you?

MICHAEL: Mary . . . Mary. These are my friends. (*Appalled at her forthrightness*) You mustn't . . .

MARY: You wouldn't know what a friend is if you had one. We're your friends, your family. What do you want these for, to hide behind is it? Whenever there's anything serious to be discussed you hang on to them like a drowning man. Why do you need them so much? Is it because reality proves too much for you?

MICHAEL: I must say I resent this . . . I won't forget it in a hurry.

MARY: (*Scorn*) You resent . . . Look at them still hanging around. Wouldn't you think they'd know better and allow us our privacy.

MICHAEL: What's the matter with you? Why do you talk like this?

MARY: Because it's true. (*Points at Sean and Jack*) These are no use to anyone. These are externals. Don't you see . . . externals. You concern yourself with these and with your wall (*Includes Moses*) and with him instead of us your family.

MICHAEL: Dammit I'm always with you.

MARY: You're here alright but you're not with us.

MICHAEL: You disgrace me in front of my friends.

MARY: If they were your friends they would have slipped away quietly ages ago and left us to ourselves. (*Suddenly turns furious on Jack and Sean and screams*) Will you get to Christ out of here and leave us to ourselves. Go on. Get out. Damn you, get out . . .

(*Jack and Sean exit hastily*).

MICHAEL: They'll never come here again.

MARY: (*To Moses*) Come on. You too.

MICHAEL: Now, now, that man is not well. (*Tips his forehead to show that Moses is not all there*) Ask the boys if you like. They know. Am I right lads? He's liable to do himself in if we don't treat him with understanding . . .

(*The boys refuse to become involved*). (*Mournfully Moses makes slowly for exit*).

MICHAEL: You don't understand Mary . . .

MARY: He understands. He knows a softie when he sees one. He knows a good touch. He saw you a long ways off.

MICHAEL: You don't understand what he's likely to do.

MARY: Do himself in is it? Don't make me laugh. (*Michael puts a finger to his lips imploring her discretion*).

MARY: He'll never do himself in. He talks too much about it. He's a slacker, a dodger. He'll bury the lot of us. (*To Moses*) Now get about your business. Can't you see you're not wanted here. This is a family. It's private.

MOSES: (*Edging to exit*) So long master . . .

MARY: So long. So long. So long . . .

MOSES: This is the last you'll see of me.

MARY: What a blessing. Now off with you. A dog would know better than hang around the way you do.

(*Exit Moses*).

MICHAEL: Why do you seek to humiliate me so much? Do you get pleasure from it? Those were my friends.

MARY: Those were the blinds you drew down in front of your eyes when you didn't want to see. Those were the barriers you kept between yourself and your true obligations.

MICHAEL: I don't know what you mean.

MARY: Of course you still have your wall but that's not enough in itself.

MICHAEL: Don't you think it's time you told me what this is all about.

MARY: That's more of it. Why should I have to tell you? You should know yourself.

MICHAEL: I'm not omniscient.

MARY: Our serving girl is pregnant. That will do to start with.

LELUM: Oh God no!

MICHAEL: Lily?

MARY: Yes Lily.

MICHAEL: Do you know who's responsible?

MARY: I'm afraid there was more than one.

MICHAEL: The little fool. Soldiers I suppose?

MARY: Yes.

MICHAEL: Another war casualty.

MARY: Your son Tom was involved in it too. He must take his share of the blame.

MICHAEL: (*To Tom*) (*Furiously*) Christ I've a mind to maim you. How could you? Look at me between the eyes when I speak to you. Lift up your head. It's true is it? . . . what your mother says.

(*Tom nods*).

MICHAEL: Speak.

TOM: Yes.

71

MICHAEL: You broke your promise to me. You have no honour, no word. You're left without a decent attribute.

MARY: You're as much to blame as he is.

MICHAEL: How in the name of God can you say that?

MARY: Long ago he should have been horsewhipped. The time of Hanratty's shed he should have been beaten within an inch of his life. Instead you left it up to me and I'm not able for it. He wears me out. I'm weary from him.

MICHAEL: Well he won't get away with it this time.
(*Looks for something with which to beat him*).

MARY: Jesus that's you all over. Closing the stable door when the horse is gone. What good is it beating him now? What worse can he do? He can sink no lower. You're wasting your time.

MICHAEL: (*To Tom*) Get up.
(*Tom rises slowly*).

MICHAEL: Have you anything to say?
(*Tom shakes his head*).

MICHAEL: You can go now, not to bed. You can go where you like and I don't care what time you come back. I refuse to be concerned about you. Go on.
(*Tom goes towards exit despondently*).

MICHAEL: Go where you like and come when you like. You're your own boss from now on.
(*Silently Tom exits*).

TONY: I don't know what good that's going to do.

LELUM: What's past is past. He's no angel but which of us is.

MARY: You tell that to Lily's mother and father.

LELUM: I know. I know but sending him off isn't going to make Lily any the less pregnant and that's what you've done, sent him off. He might not come back.

MICHAEL: He'll come back.

PADDY: I'll bet he won't.

MICHAEL: And pray who the hell asked you for an opinion?

PADDY: I'm accused of no crime yet.

MICHAEL: There's bloody rebellion fermenting here. You watch what you say. I'll not take a word of guff from anyone here. I feel like a drink. In fact I feel like going on one hell of a booze.

MARY: You'd better not. There's a lot more to be set to rights before you do anything.

TONY: What a night this is turning out to be.

MARY: I'm sorry Tony. I know it's your last night but it's better this way, better for all of us and better for the future. Let's all get our piece said. What about Lelum?

MICHAEL: I told you all about that.

MARY: You told me nothing. You made a half promise which could mean anything.

MICHAEL: (*To Lelum*) Alright. I should be able to manage to send you to university this coming October.

LELUM: I don't want to go.

MICHAEL: It will be a sacrifice but I think I can manage it.

LELUM: Other fathers with less seem to be better off. Managing seems to be no problem to them.

MICHAEL: That's because they never smoked a cigarette or never took a damned drink in their lives or never went anywhere or never ate half enough. By Christ they wouldn't buy a blasted newspaper some of them!

MARY: Their families benefitted if they didn't and that's what matters.

MICHAEL: (*To Lelum*) Look. I told you I might manage it. I thought you'd say thanks at least.

LELUM: Thanks ... but I don't want to go.

MICHAEL: You'll go where you're told.

LELUM: Come off it. You're not dealing with your school children now. I have no notion of going back

73

to school books again. I've been too long away.

TONY: It's hard when you're too long away. It's next to impossible to go back.

MICHAEL: Listen to whose talking. How can you speak about school books? You with your fine education and your experience in the civil service and all you managed to make out of yourself was a private soldier.

TONY: There's nothing wrong with being a private soldier.

MICHAEL: I have nothing against private soldiers and well you know it. What I'm saying is that you could have become an officer or a non com at least.

TONY: I don't want to be an officer.

MICHAEL: You might have thought of your parents and your family, the pleasure it would have brought us to see you with a commission.

PADDY: The pleasure it would have brought you? What about the pleasure being a private brings to him.

MICHAEL: One more word and I'll boot you so hard in the posterior your front teeth will fall out.

MICHAEL: (*To Tony*) You could have been an officer no trouble at all.

TONY: I told you I didn't want to be.

MARY: But why didn't you want to be? What's the point in having an education if you won't use it.

TONY: Being an officer isn't everything.

MARY: I didn't say it was. What I'm trying to say is that by not taking a commission you shirked. It was easier and more fashionable to become a private.

TONY: Why didn't I spend my leave in barracks with all the other misfits?

MARY: Because you're a good boy at heart and you wanted to be home with your own. That was natural but it wasn't natural for you to be a private soldier.

LELUM: (*To parents*) You two want an army with nothing but officers.

MICHAEL: No. The truth is that you dodged out Tony. You refused to face up to your responsibilities.

LELUM: (*Carefully repeating*) Refusal to face up to his responsibilities . . . I wonder now where he got that from.

MICHAEL: You're just as bad. Now that you have the chance to go to the university you back down. You probably wanted never to go in the first place. What's going to become of you? What are you going to do with yourself?

LELUM: I'm going to be an actor.

(*Michael raises his head quizzically*).

MICHAEL: You're going to be what?

LELUM: An actor.

MICHAEL: Is this a deliberate attempt to ridicule me?

LELUM: It's not. I'm serious.

MICHAEL: What crime so monstrous have I unwittingly committed that I should be visited with this revelation from one of my own flesh and blood? Be anything. Be a spy, an informer, even a pimp or a whoremaster. Dammit and blast it be a hangman but don't be an actor.

LELUM: That's what I am going to be.

MICHAEL: No man in his right mind would be an actor.

LELUM: That's because you can't act yourself.

MICHAEL: Can't I? I can act a damned sight better than many of your so-called professional actors but unfortunately I cannot afford to. I have to preserve my acting talent for my daily survival. I have none to spare for the theatre. I find that one has to act from morning 'till night in this house, if one is to hold on to one's sanity. If I gave vent to my real feelings skin and hair would fly from one end of the day to the other.

MARY: I wish to God you would.

MICHAEL: Look . . . enough of this nonsense. Have we nothing better to do than stand around here arguing? (*He locates trowel*) I have to spread this plaster before it hardens. Then I'm going to have a long drink.

LELUM: I'll be leaving in the morning.

MICHAEL: Why must you do this to me?

MARY: He's doing nothing to you.

MICHAEL: Leave us alone. (*To Lelum*) Is it deliberate? Is it your revenge for the times I've failed you? God knows I must have failed you all from time to time. I'm not a God. I'm human and I make mistakes. But each one of you would have me a failure. I'm not a failure. I have done all the things I wanted to do. I married the woman I loved. I raised intelligent sons. I suppose they had to be human too. I don't expect them to be perfect. Why then should I be expected to be perfect?

MARY: We don't expect you to be perfect and you know that well. Have I ever asked perfection of you?

MICHAEL: No . . . but my sons have and still do.

MARY: You wrong them. All they seek is fair play.

MICHAEL: Whose side are you on anyway? I'm doing my best. You've been cribbing and nagging now for weeks on end, from the first moment in fact that I started to build this wall. Secretly you're all scoffing at it. I've seen you smirk, all of you.

PADDY: I didn't mean it.

MICHAEL: Maybe not but you belittled it all the same.

PADDY: I didn't.

MICHAEL: Oh yes you did. I'm not as blind as you all think I am. This wall is not a luxury. It's a necessity. I make no apologies for building it. To tell the truth though I'm sorry I ever started it. It's brought nothing but misery. (*To Lelum*) So you want to be an actor and you're determined.

LELUM: Yes.

MICHAEL: And I don't want you to be one. However I won't stand in your way. Maybe deep down inside that's what I wanted to be once many years ago. That's just maybe. I don't know. I've never been ruthless enough in self-exploration. I carried my day. My ambitions were easily achieved. I set no Everests for myself. I had a simple blueprint, maybe too simple. But be an actor. I'll give you what I can before you leave.

LELUM: Thanks.

MARY: Let's go in. There's a chill coming on.

MICHAEL: (*To Tony*) And you Tony? Will you make an effort when you go back? You could be an officer in three months.

TONY: No chance. All my friends are private soldiers. I wouldn't be happy as anything else.

MICHAEL: You'll all end up failures.

TONY: It's what I want . . . like acting is what Lelum wants.

PADDY: And like poetry is what I want . . .

MICHAEL: Shut up you and fetch Tom.

(*Exit Paddy*)

MARY: You can't blame them for being what they want to be. It's your own fault. You were never stern. You have no right to crib if they're the same as you. It was you who made them what they are.

MICHAEL: I'm to blame for everything am I?

MARY: I didn't mean it like that.

MICHAEL: Then you had no right to say so. I'm confused enough by you as it is.

MARY: Wouldn't you tell the truth for once and admit you're creating your own confusion.

MICHAEL: Tell the truth for once? You're telling me now I've never told the truth in my life.

MARY: You're twisting my words.

MICHAEL: I am not. You're the one who's prolonging this argument. Damn you you're never wrong. It's always me. You should be christened Mary-never-wrong because according to yourself you're always right.

MARY: Will you be straight you hypocrite. Will you have the guts to take the blame just this once. You

77

are to blame for what your sons are, not me. Jesus what am I but a glorified skiv. I have no money. I go nowhere. I cook and I wash and I scrub. That's my function. I placed my trust in you to see that these boys of ours would be steered on the right course but you closed your eyes when the storms came up.

MICHAEL: The boys are alright.

MARY: They are not. You've done nothing for them, absolutely nothing. Every time a small sacrifice was needed you went out and you got drunk, or you turned your attention to something else, like the book you never finished or this wall you're at now. God you were an awful man for dodging.

MICHAEL: Now that's a terrible exaggeration. It's a wonder you stuck it so long if I was so awful.

MARY: I had to stick it for my children's sake. There were times when I would have gone but I could not leave them. It was no fun listening to your drunken promises over the years and your hopeless plans that never came to anything. I believed you at first but after the children started to come I realised I was stuck with a man who would never move out of fairyland.

MICHAEL: You kept this in a long time.

MARY: It was never too far in. I had to think of the children but the children are men now and it's time it came out. I don't want them like you. I don't want them making some girl foolish promises that they'll never be able to keep. I don't want them telling lies all their lives. You lied, lied, lied all the way through. Everything was going to be alright. You would turn over a new leaf and set everything to rights. I used believe you but Jesus, Mary and Joseph you turned over a thousand leaves Michael. I don't want them to live a lie, a dirty black lie that makes a mockery of love.

78

MICHAEL: Not opposite the boys, please — You can't mean all this. You don't know what you're saying. This isn't like you. You're shocked by what Tom did.

MARY: Maybe but if I am it's making me say what I've wanted to say for years.

PADDY: (*Enters*) He'll be along in a minute.

MARY: I started out our life in love with you but it died slowly, slowly, slowly, day after day, month after month, year after year. It died under your very eyes and you saw it die. You watched it die and you were content to do nothing about it. You dodged the reality of it like you dodged everything.

MICHAEL: You can't mean all this. If I was so awful why bother with me at all?

MARY: Some women wouldn't. They give up the fight, not because they're tired or fed up but because they just can't be bothered. It's not worth it.

MICHAEL: Tell me this? If as you say the love went after so many years what did we experience before the other children were born. Were we animals or what?

MARY: That's a rotten question.

MICHAEL: You can't answer it.

MARY: I can but it's not fair, not here and now.

MICHAEL: Tell me the truth.

MARY: I was a dutiful wife. I made a promise when I got married. I didn't go back on it.

MICHAEL: But was it love what we had or was it purely animal? That's what I want to know. It was only a travesty if there was no love.

MARY: A thing becomes a habit and a person doesn't know what it is. (*Screams at him*) Look, you don't start giving out to me, you that failed on every job you ever tried to do. I never failed you remember that. There was no escape for me. You had the pub and you had your fantasies and you had me silent, obedient and dutiful.

79

MICHAEL: Does this mean that you haven't cared over the years, that you don't care now? It's incredible. Incredible. (*Turns away, pondering, perturbed*).

MARY: I care alright. Otherwise why would I be tearing myself apart now making a show of myself opposite my children. For all the good 'twill do I'm sure. That's the greatest curse, knowing it will do no good.

PADDY: He knows now. He really does. I know him.

MARY: No. It's a waste.

PADDY: You had to do it this way. Oh he knows. I know he does. I know by his face. Here's Tom.
(*Enter Tom*).

MARY: (*To Michael*) Let's hear you now. For God's sake do something sensible for a change.

MICHAEL: (*To Tom*) Have you any sorrow in you for what you've done?
(*Tom nods*).

MICHAEL: I'll give you a letter to a past pupil of mine in Manchester. He'll fix you up with a job for the present. You can't stay around here after what you've done. Some time, some distant time you can come back when the whole thing is another sorry episode in the history of local humanity. Come here.
(*Tom comes near*).

MICHAEL: I don't find it easy to tell you go. I'll miss you more than I can say. This time, for the first time I have to be firm and I can tell you it hurts. I'm not condemning you. None of us are saints least of all me. Like Lelum's acting . . . I too have sat with a holy face in the moonlight when seduction was the highest thought in my head.

MARY: But you didn't go further.

MICHAEL: That may be so but it's all chance. Try to be a good boy in England Tom and when it's time for you to come home I'll send for you and everything will be alright again please God. Make it up with your mother.
(*Hesitantly he faces Mary. He takes a step towards*

80

her weighing his chances. She extends her arms and he goes to her).

MICHAEL: There's only one other job to do now before I go to bed. Fetch me the sledge.

(Paddy locates it and hands it to him).

PADDY: *(Alarmed)* What do you mean?

MICHAEL: That wall.

PADDY: You can't.

TONY: We won't let you. Mother speak to him. Tell him we want the wall to stay.

MARY: What's the matter Michael? What are you doing to yourself?

MICHAEL: Everybody stand back please.

(He flexes his shoulders and arms and lifts the sledge). (All stand in path of his vent).

MICHAEL: It was only a dream anyway. I knew in my heart that Fate would never let me finish it. This was inevitable. There's no other possible course open to me.

PADDY: We won't let you do it.

MICHAEL: *(Passionately, almost berserk)* It's going to be done.

ALL: No. Never.

MICHAEL: *(Shouts insanely)* Out of my path or somebody will get hurt.

(He swings the sledge. They break before him. With a cry part anguish, part relief, he assails the wall. Heaving and groaning he smashes blow after blow on it. It cracks and crumbles before his onslaught. Finally when he has exhausted himself Paddy and Tom lead him to a chair. Lelum takes the sledge and puts it to one side. Michael sits with his legs extended. They lift him to a better position on the chair.

MARY: Will we get you a drink Michael? One of the boys will go.

MICHAEL: No. Not now. He rises in spite of them and respectfully they allow his access to the exit.

MARY: Are you alright Michael?

MICHAEL: What would be wrong with me? I'm tired, that's all. I'll see you lads in the morning before you go. (*Looks at wall*). Everything will be alright in the morning. The good God always sees to that. God always comes up trumps in the morning.

CURTAIN

PROPERTIES AND FURNITURE
by James N. Healy

ACT 1 — PROLOGUE

Small table up R.C: Stool behind: old type radio on cill of window of outhouse (with practical speaker).

Window box with flowers on cill of house widow R. curtains, coloured, and also net curtains 2 upstairs window of house, and lower window at R. Water barrel RC.

A couple of shabby wooden kitchen chairs or garden ends.

(Above all stands entire show)

Wall — Prologue, as at end of show — i.e. one section, for prologue covered with green grass cloth to suggest overgrowth.

(See note below on 'Wall')

Props—off R. Tray with 4 glasses (Tony)—'Whisky'.

ACT 1 SCENE i
(Set as above — no wall)

Jack — Strong walking stick (personal).

Tom and Paddy — Strapped bundles of school books (personal).

Mary — letter from Father Cartney (personal). Stick on table (set for prologue).

ACT 1 SCENE ii

Wall one section, boarded — set stage L. of outhouse.

Shovels, pickaxes, a sledge, various bits of timber, 2 buckets, a mixing trough, gravel and sand, water.

Mary — Hank of wool (personal).

Wheelbarrow, set off L.

Shovel (Michael) off L.

Shoulder Bag: Bottle with 'meths': British Government Form (Moses) personal.

Tray with 3 Tumblers (Lily) off R.

Gallon Can with 'Porter' (Tom) off R.

Pen (Michael).

Act 1 Scene iii

Wall — as Scene 2.
Knitting on 2 needles (Mary) — personal.
Paddy and Tom — Books as before.
'Cheque' in envelope — off R. (Michael).

Act 2

Wall — First piece moved further L. "Complete piece" (which must be capable of being broken apart in last scene) replacing it directly L. of outhouse.

More of a mess than before on stage — be sure it includes 'weapons' for the drill scene. (Sean — sledge: Jack — own stick; Moses — own shovel: Michael — own shovel: Lelum, Tom and Paddy — 3 pieces of stick)

Gallon of porter set table R. also 2 glasses, Mixing trough, empty bucket, water bucket at stage L. for Moses. Football Boots and Togs in rough parcel (Tom) personal L. Football Boots (Paddy) — personal. Toy Drum set up stage (Paddy).

It is possible that the curtain would have to be drawn at the end of each 1st Act scene, including prologue, because of the necessity to change the wall: but an exception can be made between Scenes 2 & 3 which can be done to lighting.

COSTUMES

MICHAEL:

Act I. Scene I: Old blue suit and vest, shirt and tie, LDF Band on arm.

Scene II and III: Old corduroy trousers, rough shirt, torn pullover.

Act II: Change of old clothes.

TONY:

Prologue: Uniform of an officer of the Irish Army, present (or say 1963) period. Artillery if wishing to be absolutely exact.

Act II: Uniform of a private soldier of the 1943 period — artillery if possible.

LELUM:

Prologue: Dark overcoat and scarf over Act I costume (very quick change).

Act I: White open neck shirt and wide legged slacks with belt.

Act II (*a*) Football shirt and shorts (wide leg) football stockings and boots in hand.

(*b*) Revert to Act I, adding L.D.F. jacket.

TOM:

Prologue: Dark overcoat and hat, white shirt, black tie, dark trousers.

Act I: Open neck shirt and wide legged slacks with belt.

Act II: Add L.D.F. jacket for second entry.

SEAN TREAN:

Throughout: Dark suit, not too elegant, cap, white open neck shirt: L.D.F. Band on arm.

JACK STRONG:

Throughout: Not elegantly but tidily dressed in tweed suit, soft hat, shirt and tie.

MOSES McCOY:

Throughout: Dressed practically in rags — old coat and scarf: no shirt: long-sleeved, round necked white vest: old cardigan with ragged sleeves, battered waist-coat: ragged trousers and old boots or wellingtons: battered old hat.

LILY:

Throughout: Not too clean skirt, blouse and house apron.

MARY BARNETT:

Act I: Blouse and skirt with house-apron — neatly dressed. (possibly add a cardigan for Scene 2).

Act II: Same style with change of detail.

MAKE-UP

MICHAEL: Gnarled middle age with tendency to flesh: has lined fairly well and there is the slight suggestion of drink (not overdone) and of a schoolmaster. 5 and 9 of Leichner colours, with touches of carmine and greying hair.

TONY: About 24. Straight 5 and 9. Slight shading lake and grey for age about 40 in Prologue.

LELUM: About 20/21. Straight 5 and 9. Slight shadows for first scene not possible because of time — use glasses.

PADDY: 18. Juvenile.

TOM: 19. As Paddy. Possibly use moustache for Prologue.

SEAN TREAN: Rather more sallow than Jack. Was probably in the Munsters in the first war so a small dapper moustache would not be out of place. A few grey hairs at temples.

MOSES McCOY: An alcoholic. 5 and 9, with 8 worked into the cheeks, around the nose, and carefully, around the eyes, carmine can be used tactfully, on cheeks and joining to nose: also lake — but again very judiciously around the nose for veins. Ruffled hair. Lake line under eyes gives sodden eyed effect; shade lake and blue behind eyes. Script calls for full beard — a matter of choice: I didn't use one but carefully shaded cheeks with brown flecked into dark grey for stubble.

LILY: She must not be over attractive — rather slovenly and possibly not entirely "all there". 3½ and don't overdo lipstick or eyeshade.

MARY BARNETT: A fairly attractive 50. 3½ touched with 2½ if naturally youthful, shade eyes and cheeks carefully with lake and grey. Touch of white on eyebrows. If still too young, glasses will help. (steel glasses).

86

LIGHTING

Equipment varies so much from theatre to theatre that general lighting only can be suggested.

Prologue: Back Batten Blue (19). Trough at back (Apricot 14). Lights on in House stage R (51). Spots overhead confined to playing area C, and dimly on remains of Wall. FOH — light players (mainly 7 and 51) but not overbrightly. Time is late afternoon of a wintery day, moving towards night.

Act I: The bright sunlight of a June day.

Scene I and II: Blue and White in Back Batten. 14 and O.W. in trough. Mainly 51 and O.W. from overhead and FOH, with possibly some 7 Pink to give warmth. Well lit. Lights off in House; a flood off L in the alleyway.

Scene III: Coming towards late afternoon — more of a golden light. Cut down on your whites and check others from overhead and F.O.H. Check whites to necessary in Back Batten, and in trough.

Act II: Coming towards night of a fine evening in July. Blues with possibly a remaining touch of white in Back Batten. Pink and apricot, with, at the beginning of the act a touch of white in the trough. A flood of 51 from the left side of stage, fading as the act progresses represents the setting sun — (You may prefer to use 7). It catches the side of the outhouse. Lights above suitably subdued, and from F.O.H. Lights on in House. Towards the end of the play the lights dims further. At the finish. None: at the L side are somewhat silhouetted: but Michael at the door R is held in the light.

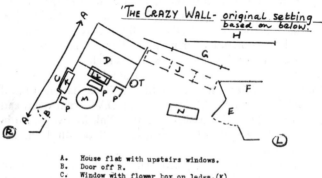

'THE CRAZY WALL — original setting based on below.

A. House flat with upstairs windows.
B. Door off R.
C. Window with flower box on ledge.(K)
D. Outhouse with sloping roof.
E. Door off L.
F. Masking piece.
G. Gate.
H. 'Hanratty's Hayshed'.
J. "The Wall" in various stages.
L. Window with ledge large enough to take old type radio.
M. Garden table.
N. Garden seat.
P. Chairs and stools.
T. Water Barrel.

There is a general suggestion of untidiness and disorder and some suggestion of wear and tear.

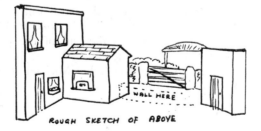

ROUGH SKETCH OF ABOVE